Power Over Panic

Answers for Anxiety

Carol Christensen, MA
Licensed Mental Health Counselor

Life Journey is an imprint of
Cook Communications Ministries, Colorado Springs, Colorado 80918
Cook Communications, Paris, Ontario
Kingsway Communications, Eastbourne, England

POWER OVER PANIC
© 2003 by Carol Christensen, MA, LMHC

First Printing, 2003
Printed in the United States of America

1 2 3 4 5 6 7 8 9 10 Printing/Year 07 06 05 04 03

Senior Editor: Janet Lee
Acquisition Editor: Mary McNeil
Editor: Phyllis Williams
Cover Design: Scott Johnson, Big Mouth Bass Design

Published in association with the literary agency of Les Stobbe, 229 Brickett Hill Circle, Haverhill, MA 01830.

Unless otherwise noted, Scripture quotations are taken from the *Holy Bible: New International Version®*. Copyright © 1973, 1978, 1984 by International Bible Society. Used by permission of Zondervan Publishing House. All rights reserved. Other Scripture taken from *The Message*. Copyright © by Eugene H. Peterson, 2002. Used by permission of NavPress Publishing Group.

Selections reprinted with permission from the *Diagnostic and Statistical Manual of Mental Disorders*, Fourth Edition, Text Revision. Washington, DC, American Psychiatric Association 2000.

Library of Congress Cataloging-in-Publication Data Submitted

To
Dr. Dan Hartman,
Steve Rinehart, Dale Hartman,
and the other Seattle-area Meier New Life Staff:

Each of you breathed
"New Life"
into the heart of a broken youth worker
and transformed her into a therapist.

Acknowledgments

Thanks to:

- Nancy Meier Brown and Dr. Paul Meier for the Meier New Life support of this project;
- Dr. Daniel D. Hartman, Psy. D., Meier New Life Clinical Director, and my former clinical supervisor, who helped develop and expand many of the foundational concepts in this book;
- Les Stobbe, my agent, for sharing with me his wealth of experience in Christian writing and publishing;
- Bruce Adair, senior vice president at Cook Communications Ministries, for his unwavering enthusiasm for this project;
- Elaine Colvin, Writer's Information Network, as well as the other members of WIN, for encouragement during the early days of my writing career;
- Mary McNeil, my editor at Cook, for investing her time and talent in a manuscript from an unknown author;
- Janet Lee, senior editor at Cook for her skillful assistance on the final phases of the project;
- The Florida Christian Writer's Conference, for providing the platform where all parties met and agreed this book needed to happen;
- Pastor Gary Stabbert and my church family at Edgewood Baptist Church for their initial encouragement to write;
- And Mother, who encouraged me that despite the black clouds and difficult periods in my life, "there would be another chapter."

Contents

Preface

The skillful author or accomplished movie director of any good suspense thriller knows when to heighten the tension—at precisely which moment to slam the door or cut the power and plunge the entire mansion into utter darkness. A master at manupulating emotions, the fiction creator has learned how to make our hearts pound and our palms sweat as we enter white-knuckled into the fantasy, enjoying the ride from the adrenaline surge. The mounting fear we feel as the pages turn fills us with the dread of impending doom. And yet we know it's all make believe. In the broad daylight of reason and logic, the manufactured sense of panic and anxiety that spilled from those pages in the night vanish like steam from a kettle. Two hundred fifty pages or a few hours later, we're all smiles again.

But in real life, people with anxiety disorders feel trapped in a life-script of gut-wrenching misgivings and paralyzing fears that do not disappear by closing the book or turning on the lights. For many, anxiety and panic are constant, chilling companions that robs them of joy, isolates them from others, causes overwhelming physical responses, crushes their self-esteem and imprisons them in a world of panic and pain.

Is this your struggle? Do you feel your life is out of control? Are you afraid to enter a room full of strangers? Are you not sleeping because you can't turn your "worry machine" off? Does your heart pound at the thought of having to speak in public? Have your fears escalated far beyond whether or not your house is clean enough for your mother-in-law?

Do you find yourself withdrawing from relationships while longing for connection with others? Do you spend a lot of time worrying about the future? Do you find yourself double- and triple-checking your doors at night to make sure they're locked? Do you wonder if you'll ever get over the abuse you suffered as a child?

If as you look into the secret places in your heart, you find your answer is "yes" to some or all of these questions, take heart! There is hope because God doesn't want you to live in the agony of anxiety. He wants to give you power over panic and answers for anxiety so that you can be victorious. Think of it! You can stop feeling out of control and helpless. You can have the power to move beyond defeat and move toward learning to manage your anxiety. A sense of empowerment can be yours.

Jesus understands what you're going through. Remember, he was the one who turned his face to the blind beggar outside Jerusalem and asked point blank, "What do you want me to do for you?" Jesus asked the blind man what he needed. It took courage for that beggar to swallow his pride and ask directly for what he needed. He knew that Jesus had the power to humiliate and shame him further. But our God is not that way! In the midst of carrying out the plan of redemption, the

Savior gave his undivided attention for as long as it took to honor one man's request.

Our God is waiting for us to tell him what we need. God honors it when we ask him for help through our prayers to him and in our reaching out to others in the body of Christ. God does not want to shame us but to embrace and empower us to face whatever is keeping us from the abundant life he has for you and for me.

Anxiety builds prison walls that keep us in our pain and isolated from loving relationships that can help free us. When anxiety becomes a way of life and rules your every move, it has become a burden that is too heavy for you to bear alone.

Jesus wants to give you your peace back, permanently; the peace that passes all understanding. "Peace I leave with you; my peace I give you. I do not give to you as the world gives. Do not let your hearts be troubled and do not be afraid" (John 14:27).

"But I'm afraid that if you look carefully enough at me or hang out with me long enough, you will see beneath my mask to uncover the person I really am," you protest. "If you find out my flaws, you'll feel I am unworthy of a relationship with you. It is too embarrassing and humiliating to admit that I've not triumphed over this. My faith must be so weak. My chronic worrying and jumpiness seem to deny the very power of God to help me overcome my anxiety. Even calling it 'my' anxiety means I've taken ownership of something so unChrist-like. I'm such a bad person God will never love me!"

A lot of people feel just like you. Some even stop going to church altogether rather than face their friends and neighbors whose faith seems so strong and whose confidence in the Lord appears unshakable.

The truth is, an anxiety disorder does not make you a bad person or a questionable Christian. It simply means that like everyone, you struggle. Your particular struggle centers around your fears and the sense of panic that distorts your view of life. Believe me when I say that God's heart is tender toward you. "Even to your old age and gray hairs I am he, I am he who will sustain you. I have made you and I will carry you; I will sustain you and I will rescue you," the Lord tells his people in Isaiah 46:4.

Having grown up in the Pacific Northwest and living there still, I love to walk the thick, towering woods overshadowed by the beautiful, snow-covered mountains. As beautiful as those woods are, I maintain a healthy respect for the power that lies hidden there. I would not want to be lost in them. But people who suffer from anxiety disorders are exactly that—lost in the woods. They long for peace, safety, and shelter. But they can't find the path out of the dark.

God wants to help you find the right path. His comfort and divine care will see you through the dark woods of worry and into the sunlit meadow of his boundless love. He sees you in full, and his love for you is not changed one iota by the particular struggles that beset you. "He who began a good work in you will complete it until the day of Christ Jesus" (Philippians 1:6). God is not giving up on you. He promises to help you find your way out of the woods so you can begin to live a "normal life" again.

That has been God's plan for you from the very moment you first believed in him. The Bible tells us he is a jealous God who will not allow a single one of his own to be snatched from him. That means you can face your anxieties from a position of great security. Through thick and thin, times of strong faith and times of puny faith, God remains solidly in your corner.

God believes in you and knows that with his strong right arm, you can experience a new freedom from doubt and worry as you learn to manage your panic and anxiety.

In the following chapters, you will learn how to equip yourself to face your foes of panic, fear, and anxiety by that same almighty power. You will be given practical tools and techniques that are proven effective in successfully managing anxiety.

"I can't," you may protest. "I've tried everything. The enemy is too strong. What's the point? Nothing has worked and nothing will!"

Time and again in my professional practice as a therapist or mental health counselor, I have seen individuals consumed with anxiety find answers that work and by the power of the Holy Spirit gain control over their anxieties. I have had patients too afraid to drive alone to my office begin to slowly come alone to their appointments. I've seen people convinced they were going to die from a panic attack learn to recognize and control the physical manifestations of their panic and return to normal lives. I've had patients who gained the power to resume normal careers. And I've seen generations in the same extended family torn apart by anxiety leave my office equipped with the understanding it will take to break the cycle for future generations. These people are living new lives. And as a Christian, you can, too. That's why I wrote this book.

In Part 1, you'll learn the difference between "fear" and "anxiety" and the most common symptoms for the major anxiety disorders. Self-discovery tools at the beginning of each chapter will help you evaluate your own feelings and behaviors—the first step in learning to manage an anxiety disorder.

Part 2 gives techniques and strategies for successful anxiety management. While many of these methods are best practiced with a licensed therapist, these chapters will provide a reference as you apply the principles on your own between appointments. These chapters will also empower you to be a more informed patient and consumer.

As you grow stronger and gain control of your anxieties, Part 3 will explain what you can expect while you move through the therapeutic process and regain the supportive community of family and friends.

Power over panic is closer than you think. It may mean long-term therapy with a licensed mental health professional. It could be a matter of learning and practicing specific relaxation techniques on your own. But never doubt that you can learn to manage your anxiety. After working with scores of individuals whom I have helped to manage anxiety disorders, I've learned there is hope!

As you work through this book, I pray you will discover answers for your anxiety and experience power over panic. It's no less than what the loving Father desires for you: "Indeed, the very hairs of your head are all numbered. Don't be afraid; you are worth more than many sparrows" (Luke 12:7).

Carol M. Christensen, M.A.
Licensed Mental Health Counselor
Meier Clinics
Seattle, Washington

Foreword

When I first met Carol Christensen, she was an intern, and I was her supervisor. Despite her being a newcomer to the Seattle Meier Clinic, she brought with her an impressive volume of experience. Working in three different inpatient mental hospital programs had laid a strong, if somewhat intense, foundation for Carol's future work with people suffering from all types of anxiety disorders. Nevertheless, her eagerness and determination to help people remained.

Carol's early counseling efforts focused on encouraging, supporting, and identifying with her patients. She latched onto educational materials that emphasized relaxation and anxiety management.

While her patients initially appreciated her gentle approach, Carol became frustrated when she didn't see the results she had hoped for. At that point, she began to realize that truth, confrontation, firmness, and limits are the balance to love and grace.

As her new style of interacting with patients developed, she also saw clearly that a single type of therapy or a simple spiritual formula was not enough to help them manage their anxieties. When she combined spiritual truth and research-based techniques—personalized for each individual—she saw lasting, life-altering change in the people who came to her for help. She saw her patients learning to live the "abundant life" Jesus promised.

The result of Carol's journey is the book you now hold. Her passion for helping others to step out of a life controlled by paralyzing fear and anxiety and into a life empowered by the Holy Spirit, filled with God's truth and love, is evident on every page.

Power Over Panic can help you face your anxiety, find the answers you need, and forge ahead to live the life God has waiting for you.

Daniel D. Hartman, Psy.D
Clinical Director, Meier Clinics
October 2002, Seattle, WA

Part 1 Understanding Anxiety Disorders

"It has been said that our anxiety does not empty tomorrow of its sorrow, but only empties today of its strength."
—Charles Haddon Spurgeon

Self-Discovery Tool

Knowledge is power. The first step in managing an anxiety disorder is diagnosis. The self-discovery tool below is merely a preliminary screening for anxiety symptoms and does not replace a formal psychiatric evaluation by a licensed health-care provider. Evaluating yourself may help you determine if you think your symptoms warrant further attention. I invite you to honestly evaluate yourself and take the first step in the journey of self-discovery that leads to freedom.

1. Do others say that you worry too much about your family, finances, career, or future? Yes___ No___

2. When you don't feel good about yourself or you feel your life is out of control, do you use alcohol, food, sex, drugs, shopping, gambling, or other behaviors to cope? Yes___ No___

3. Do you often prefer to avoid going to parties or being in a roomful of strangers? Yes___ No___

4. Does your avoidance of dogs, snakes, spiders, needles, storms, or blood injuries keep you from pursuing activities you enjoy? Yes___ No___

5. Do you avoid places and situations that trigger painful memories you can't stop? Yes___ No___

6. Have you ever gone to the emergency room with chest, arm, or leg pain, thinking you were having a heart attack? Yes___ No___

7. Have you ever felt an uncontrollable surge of fear that made you dizzy, nauseous, or shaky? Yes___ No___

8. Have you ever experienced paralyzing fright when performing in public, taking a test, or going to the dentist? Yes___ No___

9. Do you frequently avoid planes, bridges, tunnels, public transportation, closed spaces, or elevators? Yes___ No___

10. Do you often have difficulty breathing, sleeping, or concentrating? Yes___ No___

11. Do you have recurring dreams or thoughts of traumatic events in your past that still frighten you? Yes___ No___

12. Are you alarmed by exposure to germs, washing your hands more than ten times per day? Yes___ No___

If you answered "yes" to any of these questions, you will find this book particularly helpful. Read on for more information on the causes of and treatments for anxiety disorders.

1 What Is Anxiety?

When You're Panicked and Powerless

Across our country and around the world, people are suffering under the burden of fear and anxiety. In many cases, their fears have become so intense that they are crippled in their relationships with others, their ability to work is impaired, and their quality of life is so low they wonder at times if it is worth living.

There is no "instant" cure or magic pill for people who suffer with an anxiety disorder. But that doesn't mean there is no hope. You can uncover the hidden causes of your anxiety and begin your journey toward healing and restoration as you discover how to take control of your anxiety—trusting in the God who made you, learning from this book, and taking action.

As a Christian therapist, I have worked in hospitals and outpatient counseling centers with people who have experienced an acute psychiatric crisis. I have treated patients and their families suffering from a wide variety of anxiety disorders.

Within the pages of this book, you will be introduced to six fictional characters. While the characters are not real, they do represent real people—people just like you and me. These people will help you to personalize the problem of anxiety. In their stories you will discover the hope of Christ as they find renewed strength and answers to anxiety.

Fear as a Gift

From my experience, I have gained a new perspective on fear and anxiety. It is normal to feel fear when we encounter life-and-death situations. Most of us feel our hearts race and have difficulty breathing following a traumatic event. I have come to see that fear is not always a liability; it can be a gift from God during a crisis. Our fear response in the midst of danger can be empowering. Sometimes it is fear that motivates us to plan for an upcoming event or to become proactive in responding to a traumatic situation.

Anything that compels us to seek God and become more dependent on his loving nature may be viewed as a gift. That is what fear sometimes does for us. Our stubborn and independent nature often resists depending on God. But fear can sometimes do what we cannot willfully do alone.

In Exodus 14:13–14 we find the Israelites hemmed in by the Red Sea on one side and the Egyptian army on the other. They thought they were going to die. Moses assured them that God will deliver them from what they fear if they will stand firm, be still, and let God fight for them.

We can pray to our heavenly Father when we feel surrounded by life's troubles. First Peter 5:7 exhorts us to cast "all our anxieties" on him. Sometimes we face our fears by standing firm and being still—other times we must take action. In exchange for casting our anxieties on God, he gives us peace. As we grow in our understanding of God's love, we can trust in the truth of his promise in Isaiah 46:4: "I have made you and I will carry you; I will sustain you and I will rescue you."

There are some fears we all must face, and there are some fears we may never have to face. But for many people fear has moved from a blessed gift to a draining disability. Anxiety has become a heavy load they carry day after day. Anxiety that persists for a period of two to seven months or more requires the attention of a mental health professional who can diagnose anxiety and recommend a plan of treatment.

According to the Surgeon General's report on mental health, about 16 percent of the adult population have an anxiety disorder.[1] If you were to invite six of your friends to a dinner party, it is likely that at least one will have an anxiety disorder. Whether it is called panic, PTSD, or OCD, they are enduring a tremendous amount of fear, guilt, and shame.

Anxiety as a Disorder

Anxiety becomes a disorder when it impairs one or more areas of your life, affecting your ability to function at work, within the family, and in your social life. Due to genetic and biological factors, multi-symptom anxiety patterns can sometimes be found in several members of an extended family. For example, it is not uncommon for both a mother and a daughter to suffer from panic attacks.

Anxiety increases over time and

surfaces during different seasons of life. If we were only focusing on each of our six characters' reaction to a specific event like war, sexual abuse, accident, or natural disaster, we would call it trauma. But there's more to the story; anxiety is much more complex. I encourage you to follow the unfolding story line of each character in the next six chapters to understand how anxiety is planted, rooted, and cultivated into a disorder.

In chapters 2–7, each of the following anxiety disorders will be explained in more detail. Within each chapter is a self-discovery section to help you determine which of the anxiety disorders may be contributing to a loss in your quality of life. Many anxiety disorders have symptoms that overlap, so you will want to read through all six for clues as to which anxiety disorder you may be dealing with in your life. We've also added an acrostic to paint a nonclinical sketch of the disorder for the lay person or non-clinician. We encourage you to read further into the specific critical symptomology provided by the *Diagnostic and Statistical Manual* in each chapter and to contact a mental health provider before coming to any conclusions regarding a specific anxiety disorder. None of these disorders are "unfixable," but all require the training and guidance of a health care professional for best long-term results.

Generalized Anxiety Disorder

"People with this disorder usually realize that their anxiety is more

---

Generalized Anxiety Disorder

General worry you can't control

Easily tired and fatigued

Nausea or heart palpitations

Excessive distress about money and the future

Restless or feeling "keyed up"

Apprehension or fear about life

Loss of short-term memory

Internal feelings that something bad will happen

Zero tolerance for weakness

Expectations that something will go wrong

Disruption of normal sleep patterns

A fear of authority figures

Needless trips to the doctor for problems you don't have

X-raying the future

Irritability, depression, and anger

Experiences of mind going blank

Tension in muscles

Your mind becomes a "worry machine"

Difficulty concentrating

Impairment of social, family, career, or spiritual life

Sweating, cold or hot

Overwhelming feelings

Resentful of authority

Digestive disturbance

Experiencing dread and avoidance feelings

Relationship problems

Fears Associated with Social Phobia

Shouting or making a scene in public

Opening up yourself to strangers

Confronting or being confronted

Introducing yourself at public functions

Asking questions in a group or classroom setting

Letting others see your flaws

Performing, singing, or giving a speech in public

Having your private life exposed to others

Operating a public telephone or using a restroom

Becoming the center of attention at a party

Interacting with people

Accepting dates or social obligations

Specific Phobia

A phobia is a fear taken to extreme. Below is a sample list of phobias.

Speaking (glossoPHOBIA)

Public places (agoraPHOBIA)

Eating (phagoPHOBIA)

Computers (cyberPHOBIA)

Insects (entomoPHOBIA)

Flying (aeroPHOBIA)

Illness (nosoPHOBIA)

Crowds (demoPHOBIA)

Physical love (erotoPHOBIA)

Heights (hypsiPHOBIA)

Odors (body) (osphresioPHOBIA)

Blood (hematoPHOBIA)

Imperfections (ateloPHOBIA)

Animals (zooPHOBIA)

intense than the situation warrants, but they can't rid themselves of irrational concerns."[2] People diagnosed with Generalized Anxiety Disorder experience a pounding heart, an inability to concentrate, loss of short-term memory, and fatigue. "Fifty-five to sixty-six percent of the people with this disorder are female."[3] And many of the problems related to anxiety can be initially diagnosed by a trained professional as Generalized Anxiety Disorder.

Social Phobia or Social Anxiety

Individuals with this disorder have an abnormal fear of going to social gatherings where they don't know people or may be called on to perform. One of the many ways this anxiety manifests itself is through speech. Under stress in public, a person with a speech impediment will find it is more pronounced. Other individuals who are diagnosed with either Social Phobia or Social Anxiety (both are names used to describe a fear of people or various social situations) are fearful of public situations. "In the United States, social phobia is the most common anxiety disorder with approximately 5.3 million people per year suffering from it."[4]

Specific Phobia

Individuals with this anxiety disorder have a wide spectrum of fears ranging from spiders to snakes to storms. What sets these phobias apart from normal childhood fears is that they usually are irrational—they represent no real danger—and begin to impair a person's functioning and quality of life in adult years. Approximately 8 percent of the adult population suffers from one or more specific phobias in 1 year.[5] For those who suffer with a specific phobia, there is a process known as "desensitization," in which the patient is exposed in small increments to the subject or situation they fear. We will explore this concept further in Part 3.

Posttraumatic Stress Disorder (PTSD)

Often people with PTSD experience dreams, flashbacks, and intrusive memories. These vivid images are triggered by their five senses: sight, touch, smell, sound, and taste. Approximately 5.2 million people per year suffer from PTSD.[6] Soldiers, abuse survivors, victims of natural disasters, victims of violent crimes, and others under extreme stress may be susceptible to PTSD. The bombing in Oklahoma City and the terrorists attacks of 9/11 have left a wake of people suffering from PTSD.

Panic Disorder

Panic has many of the same symptoms as Generalized Anxiety Disorder, but there are more severe and acute physical symptoms that accompany this disorder. A person suffering with panic will often feel that she is choking, can't breathe, and have severe tightening of the chest. Many people who have panic attacks rush to the emergency room fearing a heart attack because their painful symptoms are so severe. Experts now tell us that "between three to six

Posttraumatic Stress Disorder

Physical reactions (all five senses) to the trauma

Outbursts of anger

Suicidal thinking

Time is frozen

Traumatic events leaving an indelible impression

Reliving past trauma

Alcohol and drugs used for a calming effect

Urgent feelings of danger that put you on guard

Mistrust of others

Avoidance of places that are reminders of the past

Trust broken in current relationships

Intrusive, recurring thoughts

Concentration and memory problems

Senses heightened or on alert

Tingling or numbness

Restricting of emotions

Exaggerated emotions, agitation, or violence

Sleep problems

Separation from reality

Disjointed memory fragments

Irritability

Startled or frightened response

Odors or sensitivity to smells

Recurring nightmares

Depression

Elevating events from the past

Resistance to living in the present

Obsessive-Compulsive Disorder

Order or symmetry

Balancing or counterbalancing

Saving or hoarding

Excessive list making

Sexual shame

Silent repetitive prayers

Illness or disease fears

Violent images fears

Excessive hand washing

Contamination fears

Overly consumed with body functions

Mistakes are intolerable

Personifying possessions as family members

Unfounded fear of anything

Lucky or unlucky numbers

Superstitions fears

Irrational fear of hurting someone

Vivid images and rumination about God

Evil-spirit fears

Dirt and germ fears

Intruding images of dangerous images

Shamed by intrusive thoughts

Overly focused on personal appearance

Rewording sentences or phrases

Door checking repeatedly

Excessive concerns about morality

Repeated numerical or alphabetical patterns

million people per year are diagnosed with panic. Twice as many women suffer from this disorder as men."[7]

But none of the disabling effects of an anxiety disorder need be permanently disabling. All are treatable, and many who once suffered from anxiety can now learn how to manage panic and lead productive, confident lives.

Obsessive-Compulsive Disorder (OCD)

Approximately 2–3 people out of every 100 are affected by Obsessive-Compulsive Disorder.[8] It can be genetic, learned behavior, or linked to other causes. For some, it is a symbolic gesture. For example, a young

Panic Disorder

Pounding heart or palpitations

Apprehension or fear

Numbness or tingling

Intense fear of driving or any specific activity

Choking feelings

Difficulty breathing

Increased heart rate

Sweating

Overwhelming sense of impending doom

Recurring abdominal pains

Dread of loosing control

Extreme tightening of the chest

Repeated feelings of being smothered or closed in

Christian woman who unconsciously believes that she is somehow responsible for her father's adulterous affair obsessively and compulsively washes her hands. Her behavior is her way of coping with her anxiety over the shame of her father's behavior. People with OCD do not find pleasure in their obsessions and compulsions, but they futilely hope they will comfort them.

As we follow our characters in subsequent chapters, we'll see how each person experiences anxiety in everyday situations. We will look at how their anxiety develops and how it unfolds over time. And we will also see their first courageous step toward self-discovery and finding treatment. My prayer is that their stories will teach you about anxiety disorders, empower you to find help for yourself or someone you love, and offer the very real hope of freedom from fear found in Christ. May this be the beginning of your journey from pain and imprisonment to peace and self-control.

Generalized Anxiety Disorder
Self-Discovery Tool

Directions: Please answer "yes" or "no" to each of these questions. (The results of this self-discovery tool are for informational and educational purposes only. Please see a mental-health professional for diagnosis and treatment.)

1. Do your family members or friends call you a "worry wart" because they say you worry too much? Yes___ No___

2. Do you worry excessively about finances, relationships, health, safety, or other issues? Yes___ No___

3. Do you attempt to avoid worry and end up worrying more? Yes___ No___

4. Do you have difficulty falling asleep or waking early? Yes___ No___

5. Do you have trouble relaxing because your thoughts race out of control? Yes___ No___

6. Are you easily frustrated, irritated, or upset? Yes___ No___

7. Do you receive adequate sleep and still not feel rested? Yes___ No___

8. Have you experienced tightness in your chest, tingling in your arms or legs, dry mouth, sweaty palms? Yes___ No___

9. Do you have problems with your stomach or bowels? Yes___ No___

10. Do you often feel "keyed-up" or live life on the "edge" ? Yes___ No___

11. Do you feel like something bad is about to happen to you? Yes___ No___

12. Do you have difficulty concentrating and have you felt your mind go blank? Yes___ No___

13. Have you experienced tension in your back, arms, legs, or other muscles? Yes___ No___

14. Has anxiety caused you to avoid work, school, or social commitments? Yes___ No___

15. Is there anyone else in your family of origin that has been diagnosed with an anxiety disorder? Yes___ No___

16. Are you a perfectionist, and do you feel that you can never measure up to another's standards? Yes___ No___

If any of this sounds familiar, there is hope and help for you. Read on to learn more about Generalized Anxiety Disorder.

2 Generalized Anxiety Disorder:
When Anxiety Rules Your Life

Why did God spare my life? Christina is asking herself again. She has pondered that same question nearly every day of the last ten years since the traumatic car accident that took her father's life but spared hers. *He must have a special plan for me*, she decides.

Fresh doubts and fears arise as she enrolls in the local college, but as she successfully completes her coursework, Christina's confidence soars. She senses that God may be leading her into full-time service, and during a telephone conversation with her mother, Sue, she gingerly approaches the subject.

"You're a very bright young woman," Sue affirms. "You have all kinds of opportunities available to you now. When I was young, my only options were secretary, teacher, or nurse. With your grades, you could be at Harvard Business School right now. It would be a great comfort to me to have a daughter—or a son-in-law—with a secure income. Now that I'm a widow, it's been a terrible struggle to live on a pension that barely covers my expenses."

Hesitantly, Christina shares her feelings. "Mom, I believe God wants me to go into ministry, maybe even to the mission field."

The silence at the other end of the telephone line says it all.

"Mom? Are you there? Say something!" Christina longs for her mother's blessing.

"Christina, I just don't see how God could be asking that of you. It sounds so … irresponsible! Are you sure you're not just overreacting? I don't think you've really thought this through."

"Oh, Mom! There are a lot of parents in our church who would give any-thing to have a child in ministry. Am I pregnant? No. Am I doing drugs? No. Why can't you just be happy for me? No matter what I choose to do, you'll never approve."

"Fine, don't worry about me. I'll get along somehow. I've been doing it since your father died and left me to raise you alone," Sue sobs into the phone. There is no way Christina can fight against her mother's tears. She has been the perfect daughter ever since her father's death—in fact, for as long as she can remember. Quietly she says she will call again soon and hangs up.

Shortly thereafter, Christina transfers to a state school where she completes her nursing degree. She goes on to graduate school to complete a master's degree. School has come easily to her so far, but a B+ in biochemistry sends shockwaves through her body. She knows this is the first step toward failure, and she has never failed before. Often she finds herself suddenly awake at 2 A.M., petrified by her unrealistic fear that she might not graduate with honors. She tosses and turns until 4, when she gets up to study. Plagued by frequent muscle and back pain, she is still surprised when one day in the shower, her back spasms so severely she can't move. Her roommate finds her slumped over the tub and calls 9-1-1.

In the ER, the doctor prescribes muscle relaxants that Christina takes faithfully. She also exercises consistently, just as the doctor ordered. Within a couple of months, she is back to her usual self.

That's when she meets Don, a strong Christian, who is studying to be a medical doctor. Christina is enthralled by his desire to eventually combine his faith with his profession and become a missionary doctor. As their relation-ship grows, she discusses with Don her fears and is delighted when he encour-ages her to graduate and pursue her calling. Christina and Don fall in love. In her mind Christina nurtures grandiose dreams of the two of them penetrating unreached areas with the Gospel and braving wild terrain like the legendary Hudson Taylor or Jim and Elisabeth Elliot.

After Christina's graduation, she and Don are married in Christina's home church. During the wedding charge by the pastor, he exhorts the couple to continue down the exciting path they have chosen: to share Christ with those who have never heard, to bring healing from disease, and to build the church in remote places. As she catches a glimpse of her mother sitting in the front pew, Christina renews her commitment to be the perfect daughter, wife, and, God willing, someday the perfect mother.

In the meantime, Don and Christina develop a plan for him to complete medical school while she works to support them. According to the plan, Don will graduate, complete his residency, and start his practice to pay off his school bills. When they are debt free, they will join a foreign missionary group and be well on their way to changing the world.

It isn't long, however, before rising education costs create a heavy financial burden that Christina tries to bear alone. She works full-time as a nurse in the local hospital and takes on short-term home care jobs whenever she can. She lives in a state of constant fatigue, but even that doesn't keep her from waking up nearly every night, worrying about how they will pay Don's mounting school bill as well as their living expenses.

Eventually Don does graduate from medical school and starts a family practice which quickly blossoms. Within three years, Christina is able to stop working and care for their new family, which now includes two children. Her worries now focus on the children. Every time she takes them out of the house, she worries that someone might try to snatch them. Every childhood illness sends her scurrying for her medical textbooks. She *worries* that they will catch a fatal disease. She *worries* that they will not make honor roll once they start school. She *worries* that they will not make decisions of faith. She *worries* that her daughter will get pregnant as a teenager or become an alcoholic or drug addict. Worry now consumes Christina to the point that she is becoming forgetful and struggles to concentrate on her daily tasks.

Don and Christina haven't been talking lately about their plans for the mission field, but Christina is confident that within a couple more years, Don will be ready to go. Still, she worries about their lack of communication and the fact that Don seems to be spending more and more time away from home in the evenings with work-related activities. According to him, there was a never-ending pile of paperwork and meetings with others in the practice.

Christina often waits up for her husband. She's not sleeping much anyway. She worries about Don's increasingly frequent late nights. Instead of understanding his fatigue and preoccupation, she becomes anxious at his vague and noncommittal answers to her questions about his work. Christina wants to think the best of him, but finds herself thinking more about the possibility that her husband is having an affair.

Then at church one Sunday, Christina notices a recently divorced woman approaching Don. The woman seems to be standing quite close. When she reaches out and puts her hand on Don's arm, Christina becomes quite agitated. *Wow!* she fumes. *That woman certainly has some "personal space" issues! Why doesn't she back off?*

Christina is troubled as well as embarrassed by her thoughts. She knows Don is a great listener and that people often approach him for free medical advice. He is such a handsome man, and she is so blessed to have him! *What am I worrying about? He's so warm and funny, that woman is just responding to him the way anyone would!*

Tuesday evening, Don is home for dinner. Christina is ecstatic! He eats with the family and plays with the children until bedtime. As Christina tidies the kitchen downstairs, the telephone rings. Unaware that Don has already answered from the master bedroom, she picks it up in time to hear a woman sobbing.

"Don, you know how my husband is. He's so mean, and he just doesn't understand me the way you do. You told me you'd keep me safe until I could divorce him. I thought I could count on you. You mean so much to me."

Stunned, Christina feels she has been betrayed! All of her worries come crashing in on her. Shaking, she hangs up the phone. *What will happen now? How can I approach Don? What about my dreams for the mission field? Should I divorce my husband? How will I support myself? What will happen to my children?*

Still in shock, she rushes upstairs to the master bedroom to confront Don with her fears.

"Oh, Christina, you are *so* insecure!" he fires back. "You're always worrying! You take every little thing and magnify it to ridiculous proportions. That caller was Tamara from church. You know how her ex-husband Jake is! Several of the men at church have told her that if he threatens her she should call one of us. And that's exactly what happened.

"Please! Do you think I'm in love with her or something? You're my wife and I love you. But you're always so edgy. You've got to stop worrying all the time."

Later, after Don has gone to sleep, Christina gets out of bed and goes downstairs. Hours later, still keyed up and wide-awake, she continues to pace in her living room. *What did I do wrong? Didn't I support him all the way through school? Didn't I set aside my education and training to raise his children? Haven't I been a good wife? How could I have been better?* Christina's mind races around in circles like an Indy car. *How have I failed him?* Her stomach lurches and rolls, and she knows she will not be able to sleep—again.

For many weeks afterward, Christina stumbles through her days. She picks up around the house only to find she can't remember where things belong. She sits down with a book and finds that she can't remember what she's read.

She tells no one about her fears for her marriage, her children, and her future.

Then one day, she forgets the baby at a neighbor's house. She meant to leave her only for an hour in the morning while Christina went to the dentist. At five o'clock in the evening, she is sitting in the kitchen trying to figure out what to have for dinner when her worried neighbor calls. Christina is mortified! How could she forget her baby?

When Don returns home that night, Christina is waiting for him. She takes a deep breath before spilling out her fears. Don tells her it is time to get help. Together they call their pastor who recommends a therapist and assures them he will pray for them.

Later that week, Christina settles comfortably into a chair in the counselor's office. She pours out all her worries as Debbie, the counselor, listens intently. After a time, Debbie explains that the two of them need to explore the possibility of an anxiety disorder called Generalized Anxiety Disorder. Despite Debbie's small stature, she exudes confidence. She reassures Christina, telling her it takes a licensed mental health counselor to diagnose Generalized Anxiety Disorder, and she has done the right thing by coming in.

What Is Generalized Anxiety Disorder (GAD)?

According to the *Diagnostic and Statistical Manual of Mental Disorders (DSM-IV)* Generalized Anxiety Disorder (GAD) is "excessive anxiety and worry, [apprehensive expectation], occurring more days than not for at least 6 months, about a number of events or activities (such as work or school performance). The person finds it difficult to control the worry. The anxiety and worry are associated with three (or more) of the following six symptoms (with at least some symptoms present for more days than not over the past 6 months):

1. restlessness or feeling keyed up or on edge

2. being easily fatigued

3. difficulty concentrating or mind going blank

4. irritability

5. muscle tension

6. sleep disturbances (difficulty falling or staying asleep, or restless unsatisfying sleep)"[1]

Some consider Generalized Anxiety Disorder a foundational anxiety disorder. It contains the primary anxiety-based symptoms that filter into the other anxiety disorders, but with specific differences. Generalized Anxiety Disorder focuses on excessive worry about the future.

Why Is This Disorder Called the Worry Disease?

Generalized Anxiety Disorder (GAD) has been nicknamed "the worry disease" because worry is the central component of this disorder. It has been said that those diagnosed with GAD have an overactive "worry machine." "This phrase describes the brain's pattern of dealing with life by conjuring up future images of disaster."[2]

You can likely guess the common causes for worry. These include finances, health, relationships, emotional safety, and a host of other issues that are important to you. The subject of your worries can change during different seasons of the life cycle.

Christina worries about lack of finances, the possibility of her husband's infidelity, her children's health, and her mother's approval. Her anxieties impair her daily life functioning, including lack of sleep, difficulty caring for her children, and impairing social relationships. This impairment is an indication of an anxiety disorder.

How Common Is Generalized Anxiety Disorder?

According to the National Institute of Mental Health, "About 2.8% of the adult U.S. population ages 18–54—approximately 4 million Americans—has Generalized Anxiety Disorder (GAD) during the course of a given year."[3] This means that if you attend a Bible study of thirty or so people, it is likely that one member will have GAD.

Generalized Anxiety Disorder has symptoms that typically peak more slowly than most other anxiety disorders, and generally, people with GAD suffer longer before seeking help. They tend to see their symptoms as reflective of a particularly stressful stage in their lives rather than as a potential disorder.

Women are more likely than men to be diagnosed with Generalized Anxiety Disorder, perhaps because generally, women more readily acknowledge a problem and are quicker to report anxiety symptoms. Men often have difficulty talking about the symptoms and are reluctant to ask for assistance from a mental health-care professional.

What Is the Connection between Generalized Anxiety Disorder and Other Mental Disorders?

People with this disease often go to the doctor for what they think are problems relating to their heart, stomach, and muscles. "It may account for almost one-third of cases referred to psychiatrists by general practitioners."[4] People diagnosed with Generalized Anxiety Disorder (GAD) are more likely than the rest of the adult population to develop other physical issues[5], including:

- Mania 12 %[6]
- Major Depression 38.6%
- Dysthymia 22.1% (low-grade depression)
- Panic disorder 22.6%
- Agoraphobia 26.7%
- Simple phobia 24.5%
- Social Phobia 23.2%
- Alcohol-related disorders 5.1%
- Drug Disorders 5.1%

Those diagnosed with GAD are also much higher users of social services and support.

- General medical 18.6%[7]
- Specialty mental and addictive disorders 19.8%
- Other human services 10.8%
- Self-help 11.0%
- Other outpatient services 38.7%

Is There a Relationship between Generalized Anxiety Disorder and Depression?

It is common for patients to have a diagnosis of Generalized Anxiety Disorder coupled with a diagnosis of major depression. In fact, one study uncovered "72% of patients suffering from major depression reporting worry at moderate or severe levels."[8]

Clinicians have speculated that the symptoms for depression and anxiety originate in the nervous system and are often similar. Some people manifest these symptoms more toward anxiety, some more toward depression, and some toward both.

Is Generalized Anxiety Disorder a Separate Disorder?

"During the 1970s researchers questioned if GAD should be categorized as a separate disorder. Further investigation uncovered that 9.6% of the people diagnosed with GAD had no other disorders, and 12% of the people diagnosed with GAD and later, other anxiety disorders, said that the symptoms of GAD came first."[9] That study cleared the way for Generalized Anxiety Disorder to be a primary diagnosis. It is now considered a separate anxiety disorder.

Are There Physical Problems That Might Cause an Anxiety Disorder?

There are a number of physical problems that can appear to cause anxiety symptoms. These can include excessive caffeine use, thyroid disease, hypoglycemia, heart disease, and substance abuse. In addition, anxiety can also emerge with other illnesses as a secondary diagnosis. It is important to go for a complete physical examination before starting medication or an intense treatment regimen.[10]

Is There a Profile of Those Who Develop Anxiety Disorders?

It has been suggested that people with anxiety disorders have a "high anxiety" personality. It is thought that these persons are more susceptible than

The High Anxiety Personality

- High levels of creativity
- Rigid thinking
- Excessive need for approval
- Extremely high expectations of self
- Perfectionism
- Competent, dependable, "doer"
- Excessive need to be in control
- Tendency to ignore body's physical needs[11]

others to develop anxiety disorders.

Those diagnosed with Generalized Anxiety Disorder or other anxiety disorders tend to have intense, passionate, achievement-oriented personalities. They learn to strive for the ideal to hide their physical, emotional, or intellectual shortcomings. They will often focus excessive attention on another person in order to camouflage their perceived faults. As a further means of hiding their imperfections, they are always on the move and ignore internal and external signals that say, "Slow down; it is time to stop."

Anxiety is a warning that your body is too stressed. It is a signal that tells your body "enough is enough." It has been overworking itself and needs time to regroup, reduce the stress, and start the healing process. Stress is a common everyday occurrence and in itself doesn't indicate a mental disorder.

Stress crosses the line into anxiety when it impairs your daily life and functioning. Most people are not instantly healed of an anxiety disorder. It is a learned behavior, a way of coping with life, which takes time to modify. Just like we don't gain weight overnight, we don't lose it overnight, either. For most, it happens slowly, over time. Experts use the term "symptom reduction" versus "symptom elimination or eradication" to describe the process of reducing anxiety.

How Does Anxiety Reduce over Time?

As a mental health counselor, my goal is to help my clients reduce excessive worry, muscle tightness, and anxiety over time. In other words, my goal is to gradually reduce their experiences of anxiety to one every two days, then one a week, one a month, and so forth. I may or may not choose to refer a patient to a physician for medication, depending on the type of anxiety and the severity of the symptoms. I would develop a treatment plan to educate my clients about healthy relationships, relaxation techniques, and a process known as "systematic desensitization." I can best illustrate this process with a story from my childhood.

How Do You Heal from an Anxiety Disorder?

When I was born, my parents lived in the city. My father owned his own business where he commercially raised flowers. I grew up with red tulips at Valentine's Day, white lilies at Easter, and pink roses for Mother's Day. Before I started school the business outgrew its location, so my parents purchased a twenty-acre farm to expand the greenhouses.

Mother was concerned because the property had a pond and I did not know how to swim. In preparation for our move to the country, she felt I needed swimming lessons as a precaution.

Every week during the summer months, Mother faithfully took me to swimming lessons in an indoor pool. I didn't like the water at first because it scared me. I had a cousin who had developed serious kidney problems as a result of a near-drowning accident, and I feared the same thing might happen to me if I started to swim.

Mother told my swimming instructor about my anxiety. He took extra care to help me overcome my fears. I learned to trust that he would watch over me. I don't think he was a therapist, but somehow he understood what I needed to overcome my fear. He started by exposing me to the water for short periods of time. I started in the shallow end of the pool and gradually swam in deeper water. Frequently, to reduce my anxiety, he told me to take deep breaths and slow down.

I remember feeling a great sense of accomplishment the first time I swam in water over my head. Mother purchased a new swimsuit for me as a positive reward. I learned to relax, and swimming became an enjoyable activity that I looked forward to each week.

One day, my instructor surprised me by advancing me to diving. My first step was to learn to jump into the water from the edge of the pool. I tried, but I couldn't do it—I was petrified. "Breathe deeply," he told me while encouraging me with his words. He told me to keep repeating to myself positive statements like "I can do it."

"I've got a deal for you," my instructor told me that day. "I know you're scared, so you don't have to jump today. You just need to stand at the edge and think of what it would be like to take the plunge. I want you to become familiar with what it feels like." Week after week he patiently waited for me, but I refused to jump. I wanted to do it for him, but my body wouldn't move when I got to the edge.

One week I overheard him making fun of me to one of the other coaches. I was crushed. I determined I would show him and save face. I refused to allow him or any other person to further humiliate me. I decided this was the big week—I'd take the plunge.

The other kids dove into the water before me. When it came to my turn to jump, I wanted to but my body froze. I got frustrated because I couldn't make my body do that simple task. I refused to step away from the edge. I determined I was going to do it—or else.

After a time my instructor gave up on me, and he turned his back to help another student behind him. I figured *this is it!* It would be easier to perform this feat without him watching me and I imagined how surprised he would be when I completed the task. Determined to avoid further humiliation, I quickly jumped into the water and instantly plunged toward the bottom. Then I panicked. I remember I felt my head go dizzy and I couldn't think. I remember gasping for breath and taking on water instead. I struggled to come to the surface, but fear had immobilized me. My body lunged from the bottom to the surface and instantly sank under the water again.

Mother saw what was happening to me and screamed for help. Because the pool was indoors, her cries were muffled so no one responded. As I came up from under the water a second time, other parents joined her with frantic cries. But all their voices together still didn't get a response from my instructor.

Mother was desperate. I surfaced a third time. She leaped over the other parents who where scattered throughout the stands. Just as she prepared to jump in the water, my instructor rescued me.

"Carol will have to continue her lessons," the wise instructor told Mother. "She has come too far to give up now. If she doesn't continue the work she has started, I'm afraid she will never go into the water again." Mother and I agreed. He did continue to work with me for several months, but I still was not able to overcome my fear.

In the meantime, we moved to the farm. It wasn't until several years after the event that I took summer swimming lessons with other kids in my new school. I had a new instructor who gained my respect and began the process of teaching me to enter the water again. He helped me to breathe deeply, relax my body and gain control over it. Eventually I learned to love swimming again, and soon I was able to conquer my fear and dive with success.

The principle I learned as a youth from my swimming instructors is similar to the one I now use as a therapist to help my patients address their anxiety issues. It is called "systematic desensitization."

My first swimming instructor began the process of exposing me to my fears in small increments. He first got me to swim in the shallow end of the indoor pool. He carefully expanded my length of time in the pool to the point where I looked forward to going swimming. Then he challenged me to move to the next level, where he gave me permission to just stand at the water's edge without jumping. When I was ready, I had the freedom to choose to jump into the water. When I jumped, I felt as if I'd failed because I almost drowned. I was ashamed and embarrassed, but I refused to give up. Still, it took me several more years to continue the process.

A new instructor was able to encourage me and help to establish a trusting relationship. With his love and support I learned to enjoy swimming and was able to dive into the deep end of the pool. With each new step I took, Mother saw to it that I was rewarded with something as a means of positive reinforcement.

There was a two-part process of helping me overcome my fear of the water. Part of the success was the technical process of exposing me to something I feared. The other portion of the equation was the love and support of Mother and my instructors. It was their caring that I believe ultimately challenged me to move forward.

Researchers have found excessive comfort and support will not help an individual with an anxiety disorder. Loving limits, however, combined with breathing and relaxation, encourage the person to move forward and take adult responsibility for overcoming their anxieties.

Love has an amazing ability to help us conquer our fears. The apostle John wrote, "Perfect love casts out fear" (1 John 4:18, *The Message*). In this verse, the word "perfect" carries with it the meaning of "whole" and "healthy." *The Message* further explains the concept this way: "There is no room in love for fear. Well-formed love banishes fear. Since fear is crippling, a fearful life … is one not fully formed in love."

People with anxiety disorders are living fearful lives, and as the apostle John acknowledged, they need love from the body of Christ to overcome and be "fully formed" individuals and develop the specific skills they need to overcome their fear and anxieties. This development is not an event, but a process. I didn't overcome my fear when I jumped into the water the first time; it was a long-term process of learning to trust others and myself.

If you have an anxiety disorder, it will take time for you to trust others and to expose yourself to what you fear. But the promise of being able to "jump in and swim" with confidence will lead you to an abundant life.

While writing this book, I had the opportunity to see underwater from a new perspective. I took a ride in a glass-bottomed boat and saw schools of brightly colored fish, giant seaweed, and coral in the Pacific Ocean. I realized there is an entire world that has opened up to me now that my fear is gone.

When Does Worry Become Excessive?

Jesus had a lot to say about worry. Early in his ministry, he gathered his followers on the mountain above the Sea of Galilee. Part of his teaching focused on the destructive implications of worry to their lives. Matthew 6:26 says, "… Do not worry about your life …" Jesus knew that worry would take precious time away from what is really important in our lives—our relationships with others and with him.

People with Generalized Anxiety Disorder have difficulty turning off their "worry machine." Some researchers tell us that the more we worry, the more we become programmed to worry. Eventually, worry can become a primary response. Simple worries about food, clothing, and shelter become excessive and consuming. People with GAD tend to worry about things that will most likely never come true.

We need to learn to rest in the Lord; to leave things we can do nothing about in his capable hands. The Bible often speaks of this in terms of "abiding in Christ." Learning to abide, or remain, can go a long way in alleviating our anxieties.

Jesus the vine likens his followers to branches of that vine. "Remain in me, and I will remain in you. No branch can bear fruit by itself; it must remain in the vine. Neither can you bear fruit unless you remain in me" (John 15:4).

Jesus goes on to underscore that "apart from me you can do nothing" (v. 5). No amount of frantic thought or activity on our part can bring about peace of mind and heart. In 2 John 9, the apostle John speaks of both the harmful consequences of taking matters into our own hands and the rewards of abiding—"Anyone who runs ahead and does not continue in the teaching of Christ does not have God; whoever continues in the teaching has both the Father and the Son."

In 1 John 2:28, the future benefit of remaining calm in Christ is readily apparent: "And now, dear children, continue in him, so that when he appears we may be confident and unashamed before him at his coming."

The more confidence I place in Christ, the stronger and more confident I become as a follower of Christ. To begin the journey of healing from an anxiety disorder, you will need to take the first step in forming a strong connection or bond with God.

Power Tools

Constant and profound worry demonstrates a misunderstanding of God and his love for us. Often our misconceptions about God are rooted in beliefs we have held for many years, probably since childhood. Because these misconceptions are based on falsehood rather than truth and steal the power God gives us as his children, I like to call them "Power Padlocks."

Study the Power Padlocks, Power Principles, and Power Passages below. Use the Power Questions to help you apply the truth to your life.

Power Padlock: "I worry about what my future will be like."

Power Principle: The same God who created us can provide for every detail of your life.

Power Passage: "'For I know the plans I have for you,' declares the LORD, 'plans to prosper you and not to harm you, plans to give you hope and a future'" (Jeremiah 29:11).

Power Question: How would my life be different if I chose to believe that God is in control of my future and his plans are good?

Power Padlock: I'm afraid of what will happen to me in the future.

Power Principle: Worry about the future hampers your efforts today.

Power Passage: "For I am convinced that neither death nor life, neither angels nor demons, neither the present nor the future, nor any powers, neither height nor depth, nor anything else in all creation, will be able to separate us from the love of God that is in Christ Jesus our Lord." (Romans 8:38–39).

Power Question: How has God shown his tender and constant love for you this week?

Power Padlock: I'm afraid I will not have enough time to get done everything I need to do this week.

Power Principle: Living one day at a time helps to keep us from being consumed with worry.

Power Passage: "Who of you by worrying can add a single hour to his life? Therefore do not worry about tomorrow, for tomorrow will worry about itself. … Each day has enough trouble of its own." (Matthew 6:27, 34)

Power Question: What do I need to help me live "one day at a time"?

Power Padlock: I've got to plan ahead so that I can have the material possessions I desire.

Power Principle: Worry shows a lack of faith in and understanding of God.

Power Passage: "Do not store up for yourselves treasures on earth, where moth and rust destroy, and where thieves break in and steal. But store up for yourselves treasures in heaven, where moth and rust do not destroy, and where thieves do not break in and steal. For where your treasure is, there your heart will be also" (Matthew 6:19–21).

Power Question: Why do I feel that material possessions can give me the security I seek?

Social Phobia Self-Discovery Tool

Directions: Please answer "yes" or "no" to each of these questions. (The results of this self-discovery tool are for information purposes only. Please consult a mental-health professional for diagnosis and treatment.)

1. Do you avoid speaking in public? Yes ___ No___
2. Do you avoid being in crowds where you don't know anyone? Yes ___ No___
3. Do you avoid social events or large group gatherings? Yes ___ No___
4. Do you withdraw from people, and do others say you're shy? Yes ___ No___
5. Do you become anxious for weeks in anticipation of special events? Yes ___ No___
6. Do you easily blush or sweat, and does your mouth get dry when you're called on in a group? Yes ___ No___
7. Do you fear doing something foolish or embarrassing in public? Yes ___ No___
8. Do you look for ways to avoid taking tests or exams in public? Yes ___ No___
9. Do your palms get sweaty when you meet new people? Yes ___ No___

If you answered "yes" to any of these questions, there is hope and help for you! Read on to learn more about managing Social Phobia.

3 Social
Phobia:
When You're Paralyzed by People

Steve opens the door to the counseling office, and a surge of fear overwhelms him. His heart starts pounding, his stomach tightens, and his face turns red. Steve's mind flashes back to his childhood when his stuttering earned him names like "retard," "dummy," and "spastic." He sighs, thinking, *Here we go again.*

Whenever Steve enters a roomful of strangers, he feels as if he is standing alone in the spotlight on a giant stage. The entire audience is glaring at him, just waiting for him to make a mistake. He lives with the gnawing pressure that he does not measure up and will never be quite good enough.

As he approaches the door to the counseling office, every cell in Steve's body seems to cry out, "Go home!" In an attempt to camouflage his anxieties, Steve takes a deep breath before entering the waiting room. Hoping to quickly find an empty chair, he scans the room and spots a beautiful woman sitting in the corner. When she senses Steve looking at her, she glances up and looks at him.

Steve tenses as soon as the woman's dark eyes connect with his. She smiles as if inviting him to take the empty chair next to her. For a moment, the thought of a possible relationship intrigues him. He longs to walk over to where she is sitting, but he knows it would just lead to embarrassment. *She'll reject me as soon as she discovers I have an anxiety problem. And even if I could cover that up, my stuttering would be obvious as soon as I open my mouth. How could a beautiful woman like her ever be interested in me!*

Steve hasn't talked much since his early teens when his speech impediment shattered his self-esteem. The pressures of adolescence coupled with his speech problem created greater and greater pain. Each negative experience Steve had reinforced his body's response (sweating, blushing, tightened stomach, stuttering) until it became automatic. These experiences and responses in turn laid the foundation for what was later to become both a communication and an anxiety disorder.

As he grew older, he worked with a speech therapist to control the flow of his words by speaking slowly. However, his strategy does not work when he is around strangers. His lips, teeth, and tongue seem to get all tangled up, and now his greatest fear is that others will notice his problem.

One of the great sources of Steve's pain is his relationship with his now ex-wife. When they first met, she thought she could help him solve his anxiety problem. As time went by, though, she got more and more impatient with him. She wanted to go to friends' houses and social gatherings, but Steve simply couldn't risk being with strangers who might laugh at his problem. He tried to share his feelings with his wife, but she couldn't understand why he didn't just "do it." She finally left him because she said he didn't care about her needs.

Steve also has had problems in his career. His mother dreamed of his becoming an attorney, but his fear of public speaking kept him from going to college. He knows that when he started working construction, his mother was bitterly disappointed.

The construction business seemed to be a perfect fit for Steve. He found success in building homes and started his own business. Whenever he had to interact with strangers, however, he ran into problems. A recent slump in the construction industry coupled with his struggle to communicate caused his business to disintegrate within a matter of months.

The failure of his business is a source of shame to Steve. *It's a good thing Dad isn't here,* Steve tells himself. He had promised his father that he would take care of the family, and having his own company seemed like the perfect way to ensure that his mother would be supported in her retirement years. Now, though, his business is gone, and he has declared personal bankruptcy as well. *I've let Dad down, and I've failed my mother as well.*

Steve's mind snaps back to the present when a baby starts crying in the waiting room. He looks at the young father who is trying unsuccessfully to quiet the child. The man's bulging biceps and his slim jeans outline an athletic build.

At forty years old, Steve is starting to lose his hair. He glances down at his protruding stomach. He can't help comparing himself with the other man who looks like a bodybuilder.

If only I looked like him, I could talk to anyone, anytime, anywhere. He takes another look at the woman he noticed when he first entered the room. *If I could just talk to her! I'd tell her how beautiful she is and how I want to get to know her better. I bet she's smart and funny and …*

Steve closes his eyes in embarrassment. *I'll never have that guy's body or a relationship with a woman that attractive. I wish I could run away and hide,* he decides. *My problems are just too big.*

Turning away to avoid having to look at the two "beautiful people," Steve notices a mother reading to her two young daughters. The older girl has strawberry-blond hair and bright blue eyes; the other has dull brown hair and bumpy skin. He has compassion for the younger one because he knows she is the ugly duckling who will never become a Cinderella.

"Mister," the younger one asks him, "what's your name?"

As Steve starts to answer the child, he suddenly feels the blood rushing to his face. The room starts spinning, his mouth seems stuffed with cotton, and no matter how hard he tries, he can't form the vowels needed to respond to the child's innocent question. Once again, his mind takes him back to his school years when he was known as "Stuttering Steve."

If I answer her, Steve begins thinking, *she'll laugh at me. They'll all laugh at me.* Steve recalls several embarrassing scenes in which he was asked a question and he could only stutter in response. He relives the humiliation over and over. In time, he develops a pattern of isolating from others, which has continued to the present.

The receptionist calls his name, forcing his mind to return to his current surroundings. He walks to the desk and silently takes from her the clipboard piled high with forms for him to complete. He finds an empty chair and sits down. After breathing deeply, he examines the first few forms and immediately feels overwhelmed. He notices the woman sitting next to him is watching as he writes. *Just like grade school! She's noticing my lousy handwriting and spelling,* he fears.

Steve's wristwatch beeps to signal the hour, startling him out of his anxious state. A dark-haired woman with a big smile emerges from another room. She looks across the room and asks for Steve.

Steve stands up and follows the therapist down the long corridor to her office. She briefly reviews his paperwork and begins the session with a question.

"When did you begin to feel fearful?" she asks Steve. Steve starts to recount a story from his childhood.

"I-I-I had to do an oral pro-pro-project for my science class in sixth grade," Steve tells the counselor. "As I was giving my report, I began to s-s-s-stumble on my words. My face turned red, my hands shook, and my heart pounded. All I could think about was getting the presentation over as quickly as possible. I was so embarrassed, and that j-j-just made things worse. I couldn't even finish. People were snickering and whispering. I just wanted to crawl into a hole. After that the kids called me 'Stuttering Steve.' Even now, years later, it still hurts when I think about it.

"Another thing that really bothered me," Steve continues, "was when my teachers looked over my shoulders when I wrote. I had terrible handwriting and spelling. One teacher in particular pointed that out whenever she could. It didn't matter how hard I tried, I couldn't make my letters look perfect like hers.

"It didn't seem to matter what I did," Steve explains. "I never seemed to fit in with my peers. When I first went to parties in college, people would start a conversation with me, and all I would do was blush. I learned to drink to cover my embarrassment. I found alcohol helped to 'take the edge' off my fears.

"Stuttering has destroyed my life. I just can't stand it anymore." With tears forming in the corners of his eyes, Steve looks at the therapists and asks "Can you help me?"

"Yes, Steve, I can help you. But I don't think stuttering is the root of your problem. My first guess is that the pain of being teased about stuttering has created an anxiety in you that's causing you to avoid people in social settings. The stuttering is simply compounding the issue."

The therapist goes on to tell Steve that she believes he has a communications disorder. But she also diagnoses him with Social Phobia or Social Anxiety Disorder. She explains to him that these are really two names for the same disorder. Steve has many questions about his diagnosis so the therapist spends the remainder of the session providing answers.

What Is Social Phobia or Social Anxiety Disorder?

The Diagnostic and Statistical Manual of Mental Disorders (DSM-IV) defines Social Phobia as "a marked and persistent fear of one or more social or performance situations in which the person is exposed to unfamiliar people or to possible scrutiny by others. The individual fears that he or she will act in a way (or show anxiety symptoms) that will be humiliating or embarrassing."[1]

The key words underlying this disorder are "humiliating" or "embarrassing." People diagnosed with Social Anxiety Disorder are fearful that someone is going to uncover their weakness. They go to great lengths to cover their imperfection by striving for perfection. Anxiety surges when they feel their weakness is about to be exposed.

"Social Anxiety is the fear of social situations and the interaction with other people that can automatically bring on feelings of self-consciousness, judgment, evaluation, and scrutiny. Put another way, Social Anxiety is the fear and anxiety of being judged, evaluated negatively by other people, leading to feelings of inadequacy, embarrassment, humiliation, and depression."[2]

Is There a Difference between Social Phobia and Performance Anxiety?

Some people call Social Phobia "performance anxiety." When they think of this problem, they think of a schoolgirl who freezes while attempting to sing a solo in a school musical. Others think of an actor forgetting his lines in the school play.

Contrary to popular opinion, there is more to Social Phobia than simple performance anxiety. People with Social Phobia are paralyzed by fear. It's not that they forget their lines, it's that they can't even go onstage. They fear that others will laugh and ridicule them. "People with Social Phobia tend to think they are less socially competent than others and they often believe that everyone notices small 'mistakes' they make. They may also greatly exaggerate the severity of the negative judgment about those 'mistakes.'"[3]

Is Social Phobia Prevalent?

Many say Social Phobia is one of the most underdiagnosed mental disorders. "Social phobia is the third largest psychological problem in the United States. It affects about 5.3 million adult Americans."[5] Some experts think as much as 7 percent of the population struggles with it.[6] This means that about one out of every seven of your friends could struggle with this disorder.

What Are the Symptoms of Social Phobia?

- intense fear
- racing heart
- turning red or blushing
- excessive sweating
- dry throat and mouth
- trembling
- swallowing difficulty
- fear of fainting
- fear of losing control of bowel or bladder function
- fear of having one's mind go blank
- muscle twitches[4]

When Does the Disorder Emerge?

About half of the people diagnosed with Social Phobia can trace their roots to a specific humiliating event. Others have said it has been with them for as long as they can remember.

"Onset after age 25 is rare, although it is not uncommon for an existing Social Phobia to remain unprovoked for years until some new social or occupational demand (e.g., meeting new people, public speaking, promotion) forces these people into social encounters that trigger the syndrome."[7]

Are There Other Problems Associated with Social Phobia?

Researchers are finding secondary problems accompanying this disorder.

• **Substance Abuse**

People with Social Phobia often turn to alcohol or other drugs to self-medicate their pain. At a social function, they use alcohol to take the edge off their fear of meeting strangers. The fear of rejection causes them to retreat to their homes, where they use illegal drugs to numb their feelings of shame, humiliation, and embarrassment.

• **Depression**

The combination of an anxiety disorder and depression is common. When an individual feels inferior, he creates a chain reaction. The anxiety causes him to isolate, which in turn accelerates depression and other anxiety symptoms. It is not uncommon for those with Social Phobia to have another anxiety disorder.

How Social Phobia Impacts School and Job Performance

"Approximately 85 percent of patients with the disorder experience academic and occupational difficulties caused by their inability to meet the social demands of securing and maintaining employment or relationships. ... Nearly one half of those with Social Phobia were unable to complete high school; 70 percent were in the lowest two qualities of socioeconomic status; and approximately 22 percent were on welfare."[8]

Steve's phobia caused him to fear going to college to become an attorney. Frustrated by his inability to communicate with his wife, his drinking escalated when his marriage ended in divorce. He fears talking with the beautiful woman in the counseling office. His construction company went bankrupt because Steve needed to talk to make bids. Others consider Steve "shy," but his shyness is only a cover for his debilitating fear.

Why Unmask the Fear of Exposure?

If you are diagnosed with Social Phobia, you are terrified that someone will uncover or reject a shameful or imperfect part of you. All of us remember turning red when a teacher called on us to answer a question and we didn't have the answer. Most of us would be momentarily embarrassed and probably do a better job of preparing for class next time.

But Social Phobia gives you a skewed perception of the event. You are deeply humiliated, believing this event has sealed your fate as a "loser." You take extreme measures to protect yourself by withdrawing from others and avoiding the class altogether.

In contrast to people with healthy fear, those living with Social Phobia have altered their lives to avoid what they consider potentially painful and humiliating situations. When imperfections are exposed, the possibility of embarrassment, shame, or ridicule is petrifying. Does any of this sound close to what you have experienced?

Steve experiences these feelings when he incorrectly forms words. His anxieties mount as he enters a waiting room full of people. He feels pressured all the time. He prepares months in advance for a dreaded social event by rehearsing what he will say and how he will act.

Students claim to have difficulty completing assignments or writing in front of others. They fear the teacher's watchful eye will note imperfections in their handwriting, grammar, or spelling. They feel great shame from their teachers or classmates when these weaknesses are exposed.

But are all fears bad? Isn't it healthy for a student to fear getting a bad grade and be motivated to study harder? When does healthy fear cross the bridge into the dark waters of a mental disorder?

What Are Rational versus Irrational Fears?

In some of the early literature, healthy fear is pictured in a scene with an ancient caveman on a hunting trip. The burly man hides behind a giant rock and comes out to meet a woolly mammoth. His heart pounds; he knows he is going to kill the monster or be destroyed by it. Fear gives his body the additional energy to act. Fear helps him lift up his arm to stab the animal and save his life. Fear can be a good thing in a time of crisis.

Many movies show fear as a tool to help someone in a crisis. I remember seeing one movie where the main character was trapped underwater beneath a car. Another character dove in, lifted the car, and freed his friend. Fear spurred this man to save the life of another. In that sense, fear helps us function in a crisis.

On the other hand, fear becomes irrational when it dominates and controls our lives. It becomes a disorder when our marriage, career, or social relationships are impaired. Because acknowledging weakness is considered negative in our culture, men and women are under constant pressure to hide weakness and appear strong.

Social anxiety breaks down bonding at our most basic level. When we avoid people, we can't bond with them. If you have Social Phobia, there is hope for you in your fear and avoidance of anxiety. To get well, you must choose to stop hiding your imperfections, learn to connect with others, and turn toward long-term healing.

How Does Bonding Heal Our Wounds?

When I was child, my family moved from the city to a twenty-acre farm in the country. There weren't any girls my age, so I began to play with my younger brother and his friends. It was a group of about a dozen boys who were mostly younger than I.

"Does she have to play with us?" I remember my brother asking Mother. She'd explain that they needed to include me because there was no one else in our area for me to play with. I wasn't very popular in this group because I was the lone *girl*. I had to earn acceptance with these boys. I became a tomboy and learned to run and climb trees like them. With my self-esteem on the line most of the time, I looked for ways to triumph over the boys as often as possible.

One day I got the idea to ride bikes for a competition. *I know I can win that one*, I thought. I taunted the leader of the pack until he got tired of saying no to me. The boys couldn't stand being challenged by a *girl*, so they finally agreed to let me race their leader, the biggest bully of the bunch, down an old gravel road.

I had practiced riding my bike for some time because I was determined to win. The day of the big race came; I mounted my bike, already certain of my victory. The red flag went down, and I was off like a shot. I managed to gain half a bike length on the others. *The victory is mine!* I imagined.

At that moment, the bully leaned over and, with a wicked grin, pushed my bike to the ground. I tumbled over and skidded across the gravel and dust. My shorts were filthy and my knee was dripping blood. I stood up, brushed myself off, and hid my face in my jacket, so the boys wouldn't see the tears that threatened to spill.

I limped back to the house, calling for my mother. My wounded knee wasn't nearly as painful as my hurt pride, but Mother could only tend my outward scrapes. She went to the medicine cabinet and took out some rubbing alcohol to apply to the wound. When she applied the medicine, I let go and screamed loud and hard.

A few days following the accident, I noticed a scab had formed on my wound. Later that afternoon, while playing goalie at a soccer game at school, another student went to kick the ball, missed, and hit my knee tearing open the scab. My teacher insisted I go to the school nurse who looked at my knee and grimaced. Going to her first-aid kit, she got out a pair of tweezers, and "operated" on my knee. A few moments later, she pulled out a relic from the bike race: a small piece of gravel.

"Your knee would never have healed if we hadn't gotten this out," the nurse told me. I wasn't a therapist yet, but I learned an important lesson about healing that day.

Before God can heal the broken parts of our hearts, he must remove the smallest piece of gravel that impedes our healing. Although painful at times, the "surgery" must be endured.

For people with an anxiety disorder, avoidance is the gravel that must be removed. The avoidance needs to be acknowledged and brought into the light of a loving relationship with God and others. From the beginning, God intended it to be so.

What Is the Biblical Foundation for Bonding?

In the opening pages of the Bible, we find a garden paradise where people could be honest with God and each other. Adam and Eve were created in perfect love—they didn't need to doubt their identity nor did they question their completeness. When they ate the fruit and sinned, the bond of understanding was broken and communication was severed—an eternal separation emerged.

Rather than restoring the tattered relationship, they established an unhealthy pattern of isolation and avoidance. Adam blamed Eve, Eve blamed the serpent, and the first couple hid from God. As their descendants, we have inherited their sin. Our ability to love has been tainted by deception, control, and manipulation.

How Does Sin Destroy Bonding?

God originally designed us to connect with others, but now sin contaminates all human relationships. As a result of the Fall, we have inherited injured parts that are too proud and fearful to seek love from others. Our pain and distress cause us to avoid relationships. Paradoxically, we need love, but we fear love. We long to embrace it but don't know how, so instead we run from it and push it away.

Even as we run, however, we experience the anxiety of loneliness and isolation. When anxious people avoid relationship, their behavior leads them to more extreme patterns of avoidance. To fill their emptiness and God-given need for relationships, they settle for cheap substitutes. They try to control and conceal their need through addictions such as alcohol, drugs, sex, and gambling. But these substitutes only connect them with a love counterfeit. In time, they despair, lose hope, and their broken hearts become hardened.

How Can You Break Your Cycle of Pain?

The ability to open your heart and accept love has been compared to a rosebud. The rosebud is closed until the petals are exposed to God's sunlight. With time and love, the rose comes to full bloom. The warmth of the sun increases the depth and hue of each rich red, yellow, or pink petal and releases the beautiful aroma within. Receiving love from others can add rich color and a fragrant aroma to your life.

A simple yet difficult way to stop destructive patterns is to open your heart and ask for love. When we have been deeply wounded, we have great difficulty risking love again. Some of us are good at caring for others, but we have difficulty accepting love ourselves.

I often talk about giving and receiving love to my clients in marriage counseling. I've yet to have spouses acknowledge their need for love and immediately agree to ask for it from their spouses. Usually, their faces turn white, their eyes widen, and they look toward each other in terror. They can't imagine being so vulnerable as to tap their partner on the shoulder and say, "Honey, please love me."

How Can You Learn to Receive Love?

Risking receiving love may be the most difficult, but most critical, struggle for the socially phobic person. Anxiety sabotages all hope of getting the love they need.

It is difficult for others to understand what we need, because we can't read each other's minds. We have to be forthright and honest, even though our tendency is to repeat the pattern of blaming and hiding that Adam and Eve established.

Every person is different. We need to understand that individuals have different preferences about how they want to be loved. Words and touch are two primary means of establishing a connection with another person. When words have no meaning for some people, touch can also be used as a means to communicate emotional support.

Those who've had an abusive or negative sexual experience need to learn to separate healthy touch from unhealthy touch. Good touch always has good boundaries. A comforting hug, a touch on the arm, or a pat on the shoulder can show support beyond what words may express to a brother or sister in pain. To be responsible, we must risk asking for the kind of love we need.

What Are Specific Ways to Ask for Love?

Our sin nature makes it hard to ask others to meet our needs. But when you are in pain, don't be afraid to ask for

- Prayer;
- Healthy physical touch on the arm or shoulder;
- Words of encouragement and comfort;
- Feedback on your strengths and weaknesses;
- A listening ear to hear feelings, thoughts, and dreams;
- Opinions of a valued and trusted friend;
- Hugs from a Christian brother or sister;
- Acceptance, comfort, value;
- Others to like us and care for us;
- Time from another person to help with daily activities during crisis.

No inspired writer has more to say about the value of our individual contributions to God's plan than Paul. In 1 Corinthians 12:27, he boldly states, "Now you are the body of Christ, and each one of you is a part of it." In verse 18, he makes it wonderfully clear that whatever part you've been called to play, you are known and needed: "But in fact God has arranged the parts in the body, every one of them, just as he wanted them to be."

Better read that again.

"You mean that with all my insecurities, I"m still important to the church?" Of course you are.

Allow the healing in worship to bind up your wounds and soothe your hurts—for a time. Then as you bond with others and form relationships, you may find ways to help others who are hurting. You may be surprised to discover that you are most ministered to as you minister to others.

It's fine to ease into it at first. You might do a little low profile volunteering to mow the church lawn or be the women's group treasurer. Perhaps you could be a "minister of hugs" where few words are required to express God's love.

If you are serious about trying to connect with others when your instinct is to avoid and flee, remember: Someone out there needs what you have to give and can benefit from your experience. Befriending that person takes your mind off yourself and your anxieties and refocuses your energies on the help you can give. As they blossom from your attention, see if you don't as well.

Power Tools

Power Padlock: I'm afraid to ask someone to love me—they will hurt me in the same way all the others in my life have injured me.

Power Principle: God designed us to need love and to reach out to others for our needs.

Power Passage: "But if we love one another, God dwells deeply within us, and his love becomes complete in us—perfect in love!" (1 John 4, *The Message*).

Power Question: Look back at the list of ways to be loved in this chapter. What are some tangible ways I can ask others to love me today?

Power Padlock: If I let people love me, I'm afraid they will know who I really am and eventually reject me.

Power Principle: Love demands that we have to let go of our pride, independence, and stubbornness to be vulnerable to one another.

Power Passage: "Well formed love banishes fear" (1 John 4, *The Message*).

Power Question: What weaknesses or shortcomings make me feel I'm unlovable? From the list of needs provided in this chapter, how am I willing to put down my guard and let someone love me despite my weaknesses today?

Power Padlock: If I love and serve others, isn't that enough to fill the void in my heart for love?

Power Principle: We need to learn to let others love us before we can give healthy love to others.

Power Passage: "We love because he first loved us" (1 John 4:19).

Power Question: Why do people often confuse healthy love with an unhealthy taking care of others? How can I use the above list to help me avoid taking care instead of giving and receiving love?

Power Padlock: If I ask someone to pray for me, that person will think I can't handle my problems.

Power Principle: Sharing each other's burdens is a big part of being in relationship—with friends, with family, and with other believers.

Power Passage: "Carry each other's burdens, and in this way you will fulfill the law of Christ" (Galatians 6:2).

Power Question: Who can I trust to pray for me about a problem I'm facing now?

Specific Phobia Self-Discovery Tool

Directions: Please answer "yes" or "no" to each of these questions. (The results of this self-discovery are for information purposes only. Please see a mental-health professional for diagnosis and treatment.)

1. Are you fearful of dogs, snakes, spiders, rats, or other animals? Yes ___ No___

2. Do you avoid elevators, public places, or closed spaces? Yes ___ No ___

3. Are you fearful of water? Yes ___ No___

4. Do you avoid traveling across bridges or through tunnels? Yes ___ No___

5. Are you afraid of accidents, blood, or an invasive medical procedure? Yes ___ No___

6. Do you fear flying, using public transportation, or driving? Yes ___ No___

7. Are you afraid of choking, vomiting, or becoming ill? Yes ___ No___

8. Do you tend to get anxious during a storm or a change in the weather? Yes ___ No___

If you answered "yes" to any of the questions above, please continue on to questions 9–11. When answering these questions, please reference your answers to the fears listed above.

9. Do you think that your fear of these items is irrational? Yes ___ No___

10. Have you significantly altered your career, family, or social relationships to accommodate your fears? Yes ___ No___

11. When you anticipate seeing these objects or doing any of the activities listed above, do you experience immediate fear of anxiety and seek to avoid them? Yes ___ No___

If you answered "yes" to any of these questions, there is hope and help for you. Please read this chapter on Specific Phobia.

Disgust envelops Sarah, and she hurriedly turns away from the mirror. She feels very uncomfortable in this unfamiliar building. Why can't she just go home? Sarah has a habit of holing up at home to avoid public scrutiny. On the rare occasion when she does go out, she tries to conceal her ample frame with outdated, oversized clothing.

Hoping that the mirror had been mistaken the first time, Sarah risks another look. As she evaluates herself in the mirror, she sees that the small-framed woman with the poodle is looking at her too. *How can she even stand to look at me? I look like a freak! When I get home, that's it! I'm never leaving the house again!*

Thankfully the elevator stops on the tenth floor to let out the intimidating woman and her dog. Relief washes over Sarah when they are gone and she is alone again. Then she notices the perspiration-soaked armholes of her oversized cotton camp shirt. Her navy-blue, polyester pants are stuck to her large thighs, and her swollen ankles protrude from the sides of her white summer sandals.

How did I let myself get like this? Moisture forms in the corners of her green eyes. In her mind Sarah goes back to the day she got married and was able to slip into her slim size-6 wedding gown. Her silky blonde hair had been styled to frame her rosy skin. Her makeup was applied to highlight her beautiful eyes. Her family and friends said that she looked like a princess with her long train cascading down the steps of the altar as she said her vows. And she felt it! It had been a perfect day.

That night, however, was another story. Sarah's expectations of her wedding night were dashed when she found herself unable to respond to her husband. After the honeymoon, any hope of fantasy was soon replaced with reality. Three children in four years left her little time to care for herself. Her life became a blur of endless piles of laundry, dirty dishes, and multiple trips to the grocery store each week. She took pride in meeting the physical needs of her family and even volunteered to be a room mother, troop leader, Sunday school teacher, and carpool driver. All this activity earned Sarah the elementary school "volunteer of the year" award, but from that point forward her relationships with friends and family began to disintegrate. Now, with her children grown and gone, Sarah and her husband have little reason to communicate, her friends seldom drop by, and her children seldom call. It seems that everyone else's life has meaning and purpose, while hers is empty and wasted.

I hate what I've become, she reflects. *I'd die if anyone knew the "volunteer of the year" doesn't have any friends—she barely has a marriage—and her children never call and thank her for all she's done for them.*

My life just isn't working. When did I lose control? Sarah remembers her childhood fear of dogs. She recalls losing it when her son accidentally cut his finger with a butcher knife. It had turned out to be a minor cut but all that blood

4 Specific Phobia:
When You're Petrified of Things

There is no way out. Sarah panics as the elevator doors close tightly behind her. She is on her way to her first appointment at the counselor's office—on the thirtieth floor.

I'm trapped! she imagines. A vague sensation of feeling closed in and uncomfortable in a new environment is overtaking her. *I've got to get out of here. I just know something bad will happen; I need to go home!* Her heart rate accelerates—she gasps for breath.

What if the elevator gets stuck? What if I can't get out? What if ... ? Sarah attempts to slow down her runaway thoughts and reassure herself. She inhales deeply and exhales slowly. *I'm being ridiculous! How many people do I know who've ever been trapped in an elevator?*

Sarah's conversation with herself is interrupted when the elevator doors open and a trim, well-dressed woman carrying a fluffy, white poodle enters. When the dog sees Sarah, it barks and struggles to get out of the woman's arms. Sarah shivers as she recalls her childhood fear of dogs. Although she has outgrown many of her other grade-school phobias, she still struggles with her response to animals.

Sarah's attention shifts to the mirror in the back of the elevator. The sight of her reflection makes her frown. She can't help but notice how under her oversized blouse her pants outline every bump and bulge. *I look terrible! Tha⟨ woman must think I'm a total slob. Oh! And my hair! I can't even remember t⟨ last time I had my roots touched up. I can't believe I even had the nerve to leave ⟨ house. This is so embarrassing!*

was horrifying. Now with the onset of menopause, she feels even more anxious when she is in a closed-in or high place, or driving through the tunnel near her home. Her fears have steadily increased to the point that she can't ride in airplanes, drive over bridges, or climb stairs without feeling petrified.

My entire life is a mess. My husband thinks I'm nuts. He says, "How can a grown woman be so afraid of everyday things—snakes, spiders, stairs, elevators?" It's not like Sarah hasn't asked herself these questions. In fact, many times she has rationalized: *My mother, grandmother, and great-grandmother were afraid of those things too; I can't help it. It runs in the family.*

Sarah finds herself gripping the rail in the elevator as her thoughts continue. *My friends think I'm crazy, too. They don't call very much anymore, and they don't understand why I never want to go anywhere. They say my staying home all the time is "irrational." I've never really been able to talk freely about my fears with them—maybe they're not my friends after all—I guess I really don't have any friends.*

Ding! Sarah breathes a sigh of relief when the elevator door finally opens on the thirtieth floor. As she enters the counselor's office, she resolves to work on her fears. To begin the session, Sarah tells Debbie a lengthy story about her childhood.

"I was four when my family moved to a farm. One of my greatest problems in transitioning from city to country life was the big, scary dog that ran free in the neighborhood.

"'Can't we please move back to the city?' I begged my parents.

"'You need to learn to deal with your fears,' Father told me.

"I protested, but Father held lovingly and firmly to his position: 'You'll have to overcome your fear of dogs.'

"I knew I couldn't do that. I knew that one of these days, the dog was going to come after me. I had seen the dog snapping at other children, and I knew it was only a matter of time before those big white teeth would be clamped onto my leg. I found myself listening for his ferocious bark whenever I was outside. I even dreamed about him. Soon I forgot about the move from the city to the farm, making friends at school, or doing chores. Instead I spent great amounts of time worrying about the dog.

"It wasn't long before my feelings about the neighbor's dog grew to include all dogs. I hated big ones, medium-sized ones, and even small ones.

"I knew I had a big problem; everyone in our rural community had a dog. There would be no escaping them as long as we lived on the farm. I felt so dumb. *This is stupid. Why can't you just get over your fear of dogs?*

"My fear was so pervasive that my parents and others in our community became quite concerned. An older man in the community suggested that my parents get me a pet collie thinking my negative thoughts about dogs could be overridden by positive experiences with them.

"My parents got the dog, and I got angry. Didn't they understand? I DIDN'T LIKE DOGS! I was terrified and wanted nothing to do with this new pet.

"Well, they could buy the dumb dog, but I didn't have to like her. In fact, I chose to completely ignore her. I often escaped to my bedroom and stayed there for hours. In my room, no one pressured me and I didn't have to deal with my problems.

"My parents were stymied by my response, but finally they gave up. I was rather stubborn as a small child, and I simply refused to let go of my fear. I decided I would just live with it.

"Of course, if I had been able to 'just live with it,' I wouldn't be here today. My childish fear of dogs seems to have grown into so much more.

"When I was about twenty, I developed a fear of tight spaces, tunnels, flying, and driving.

"During that time, I worked in the computer software industry and did very well. I was offered a significant promotion, but the new job required that I travel. I turned down the job because I was just too afraid to fly. A year or so later, I got married and became a housewife and mother. I often wonder how my life would have been different if I'd overcome my fears.

"I want to go back to work," Sarah confides in Debbie, "but I'm too afraid. I could hardly force myself to come here today. Still, there's nothing for me at home. My children are raised—I'm no longer needed—I feel there's no purpose left in my life—and the Lord might just as well take me home." She pauses a moment before starting to cry. She looks at the therapist and opens her mouth to plead for help, but nothing comes out except sobbing.

Debbie feels compassion for Sarah. She asks her a number of technical questions that help her differentiate between anxiety disorders. People with Sarah's symptoms can diagnostically fit into a number of categories: Specific Phobia, Posttraumatic Stress Disorder, Agoraphobia, and Panic. Based on Sarah's answers to Debbie's questions, she diagnoses Sarah's problem as Specific Phobia. Sarah's specific fear of going outside is called Agoraphobia.

Sarah's eyes widen and her hands shake when Debbie reveals her diagnosis. A sense of relief sweeps over her: someone understands. Sarah is not alone. She immediately has a number of questions about her new diagnosis.

What's a Specific Phobia?

Only a mental-health-care professional can diagnose the disorder once known as "Simple Phobia," now called "Specific Phobia." According to the

Diagnostic and Statistical Manual of Mental Disorders (DSM-IV), "The essential feature of Specific Phobia is a marked and persistent fear of clearly discernible, circumscribed objects or situations. Exposure to the phobic stimulus almost invariably provokes an immediate anxiety response."[1]

The Surgeon General says, "Approximately 8 percent of the adult population suffers from one or more specific phobias. ..."[2] Several experts feel the criteria for Specific Phobia is too limiting. Others claim it is more accurate to say, "Specific phobias strike more than 1 in 10 people."[3]

Specific phobias range from amathophobia (fear of dust) to zelophobia (fear of jealousy). An extreme fear (anxiety) becomes a phobia when a person's life is controlled by the feared object or situation. Phobias usually develop in childhood but can develop at any point in life.

What's Anxiety Got to Do with It?

Specific Phobia isn't diagnosed when a child is simply afraid of snakes, but only if the specific fear becomes an anxiety and impairs daily activities at school or with family. It becomes a disorder when the child structures his life to avoid snakes. For example, the child is unable to go to school or go on a family camping trip because he is afraid he might see a snake.

Another example is the student who, because of her phobia of cockroaches, refuses a scholarship to a college in Florida. The anxiety is irrational because it stops her from achieving her lifelong goal of securing a college degree.

"Phobias are not just extreme fears," one professional explains. "They are irrational fear of a particular thing."[4] These fears dominate and determine lifestyle choices for people diagnosed with Specific Phobia.

The means of avoiding a person's fear can be extreme. Some people, like Sarah, are unable to take a promotion because it would mean travel. Others must live on the plains because they are anxious about living in the desert where they might see snakes. And still others are irrationally fearful and anxious about going to work because they must cross over a bridge.

Sarah's childish anxiety about dogs, her irrational reaction to her son's blood injury, and her current phobia of elevators highlight the far-reaching consequences of this disorder. Though no specific event triggered these reactions in Sarah, her growing anxiety is reflected in the way she lives each day.

What Are the Categories of Phobias?

There are five basic categories of phobias representing a wide range of irrational fears that paralyze people.

1. Animal type: cued by animals or insects
2. Natural environmental type: cued by objects in the environment, such as storms, heights, or water
3. Blood/injection/injury type: cued by witnessing some invasive medical procedure
4. Situational type: cued by a specific situation, such as public transportation, tunnels, bridges, elevators, flying, driving, or enclosed spaces
5. Other type: cued by stimuli other than above, such as choking, vomiting, or contracting an illness

What Is Agoraphobia?

One of the best known of these specific phobias is agoraphobia. The term *Agoraphobia* comes from the Greek and means "fear of an open marketplace."

People with this disease are afraid to go out in public, so they hide or isolate themselves from others. Sarah's case might be specifically linked with Agoraphobia and a host of other phobias. Agoraphobia is frequently triggered by Panic. (Panic is discussed in another chapter.) They fear having heart-attack-like symptoms in a public place and so will refuse to leave their homes except when absolutely necessary. They may go grocery shopping in the middle of the night to avoid seeing other people.

People with Agoraphobia are petrified they will be abandoned by family or significant others. Their greatest fear is that they don't deserve to be loved. Many who suffer from this disorder are fearful because few people have connected or bonded with them, and one or more vital connections have been broken, most often in childhood.

For example, if a mother is hospitalized—even for a short time—or leaves the home permanently because of divorce or death, a child may develop a fear of abandonment that could become a phobia of surgery (topophobia), illness (nosophobia), doctors (iatrophobia), or being alone (monophobia).

Will You Outgrow a Phobia?

According to the Surgeon General, phobias begin in childhood. For most, there is generally a second peak around age 25.[5] The symptoms and intensity can vary according to stress levels at home, at work, or within other relationships. Once a phobia takes hold, most people need treatment to find long-term healing.

Sarah's visit with the therapist is her first step in the healing process. She feared dogs in her childhood, and in her twenties, she feared flying. When her children left the nest, her phobias resurfaced but in a different form—she developed a fear of elevators and tunnels.

Sarah's progression is fairly common. As a person gets older and takes on new responsibilities at different stages of life, her fears often take on new or extended forms.

Does Specific Phobia have a Relationship to Traumatic Events?

It's important to understand that Specific Phobia is not related to a traumatic event in the sufferer's life. In Sarah's case, her fear of elevators wasn't triggered by her being stuck in one or by a friend dying in one. If her fears *had* related to a single traumatic event, she probably would have been diagnosed with Posttraumatic Stress Disorder or Panic. Posttraumatic Stress Disorder is associated with flashbacks or dreams of a specific traumatic event like war, an accident, or childhood abuse.

Is There a Connection between Specific Phobia and Panic?

Telling the difference between these disorders is tricky, and an expert diagnosis is required. A Specific Phobia can merge with other anxiety disorders, such as Panic. That means that when someone has Agoraphobia and Panic, for example, he may experience severe physical symptoms such as chest pains, choking, or difficulty breathing when he leaves his home.

Is There a Family or Cultural Connection?

There is much speculation about the role of the family in this disorder. Phobias may run in families, but therapists aren't sure if they are genetic or learned behaviors. For example, if your mother was or is afraid of spiders, it is likely that you'll be afraid of spiders—even if you've never had a frightening or painful experience with them.

Even outside our families, we can be influenced to fear certain things. If we hear that someone has been bitten by a snake, for example, we become afraid too. Or, if we hear of a bridge collapsing, we may change our route to church or school to avoid having to cross any bridge. Still, almost no one is afraid of cars, even though almost everyone has experienced or witnessed a car accident in which someone was injured. Some people may be inherently "prepared" to learn certain phobias.

From culture to culture, there appears to be some differences regarding how these fears emerged. Agoraphobia is more common in the United States than in Europe, and in Japan, the fear of offending someone is widespread. Professionals aren't sure why fears vary from place to place, but many think that they develop as a learned behavior to cope with each culture's pace and lifestyle.

How Does Bonding Apply to Specific Phobia?

Bonding through relationships is a critical part of the treatment for anxiety disorders. You can start this process by speaking your fears to another person and seeing that person's perception of your fears. Many of my clients in therapy groups feel that no one has experienced what they've endured. They are often relieved when they find that other group members have experienced similar pain. When you know that others accept you despite your weaknesses, healing will follow.

If you've been hurt, it's natural to withdraw from others to protect yourself. In order to get the acceptance you want and need, however, you must take this important first step of asking for help to grow up emotionally; we can't heal alone.

Psychologists tell us that the process of bonding begins at conception, continues in the womb, and grows until we enter the world as a helpless baby needing a mother's milk to survive. An attachment is formed between child and mother when Mother looks down at her precious child, and the hungry baby learns that Mom can provide the nourishment he needs. This in turn unlocks the emotional and physical growth process.

The process of bonding does not end when we are out of diapers. We never outgrow our need for love, and as healthy adults we connect to our mates, children, and friends.

When we deny these needs and don't connect with others, we create problems for ourselves by forming unhealthy attachments. These unhealthy attachments include alcohol, drugs, gambling, food, work, and sex. When we bond with these replacements, our God-given needs for companionship and attachment are not met. Until we choose to enter into relationships that are based on having our needs met and meeting the needs of others, we will not be able to overcome our fears and move beyond them.

Once we do make the choice to seek relationships, we will need to establish healthy boundaries. These boundaries will define, protect, structure, and set limits on how quickly we move into a friendship.

For example, your new friend may want to see you Friday night, Saturday night, and Sunday afternoon. You may have other obligations or simply need time to yourself. As a healthy adult, you might have to say "no!" or suggest an alternative. This is good! Don't be afraid to balance your needs with those of the other person. If you don't, you'll soon find yourself again tangled up in an unhealthy pattern of relationship.

There are unhealthy or "unsafe" people who get their love needs met by rescuing others and controlling them. If you find yourself in a relationship where your "no" is not respected—get out of this unhealthy care-taking relationship! Seek God's wisdom in discerning the difference between care-giving safe people and care-taking people who will be unsafe for you.

Start slow.

Start smart.

But start!

Long-term healing comes when we establish close relationships with people who risk bonding with us and telling us the truth. We need to hear truth from those who love and care about us and will not manipulate or control us. If you've been hurt by what you thought was love in an unhealthy relationship, I urge you to taste the goodness of grace in small bites—open the damaged, broken parts of your heart slowly to God and others.

Why Are Love and Truth Needed?

The balance between love and truth is difficult. Too much love or truth without love can be destructive to a relationship. Most of us can only tolerate truth in small doses. We don't look forward to sitting down for a cup of coffee with a friend and having them tell us ten things that are wrong with us. However, if a friend lovingly shares a concern with you, there is potential for you to experience growth and maturity.

Truth can be compared to a piece of tough stew meat. If you try to eat it by itself, it is hard to swallow and you can easily choke. But when a chef takes the same piece of meat, cuts it into small pieces, seasons it with meat tenderizer (love), mixes it with onions and carrots (loving relationships), and lets it simmer on the stove (time), it gains a savory flavor.

We need extended loving truthfulness mixed with caring relationships in order for our injured and anxious parts to be healed. Loving again is hard when we've been severely wounded. Allowing ourselves to be vulnerable and loved by "safe people" is a process that takes time, but it starts with what we call "fellowship."

How Does Fellowship Apply to a Specific Phobia?

In the Bible we are taught that when we confess our weaknesses and sins to others, we are healed. The spiritual principle this concept flows from is called "fellowship." Many of us have a misunderstanding of this biblical term. It does not mean going to church and scrambling for the door when the pastor says "Amen!"

Real fellowship means that we share the deep, dark parts of our hearts with another person. It means we no longer need to hide, manipulate, or cover up our imperfections. We can be free to show our flaws to safe people without fear of rejection. The ability of others to love us, despite our failures and imperfections, is a manifestation of God's love.

The apostle Paul understood weakness. Many theologians think Paul was a homely man. Although there is controversy regarding what made him ugly, many speculate on what it might have been. Some think he had an eye problem that sent puss streaming down his face. Others think he was overweight or short. Paul did not try to conceal his affliction nor did he isolate himself from others. In fact, just the opposite is true! Like Paul, people with phobias need to be honest and direct about their pain and anxieties versus hiding them in shame and humiliation.

Three times Paul asked the Lord to take away his "thorn in the flesh." God heard Paul's plea and responded, "My grace is sufficient for you. My power is perfected in your weakness" (1 Corinthians 12:9). That is God's word to you as well.

How Do We Gain Power to Love in Truth?

Love is a powerful tool for healing our weaknesses and coming to terms with our anxieties. When we accept our shortcomings and bring them into the warmth of God's love and truth, we receive dynamic power for loving others and ourselves.

When Adam and Eve withdrew and tried to hide their needs behind a fig leaf, God sought them out. They feared God would see their shortcomings—their "badness." God met their fear with love and truth to restore their relationship.

We look at their pitiful attempt to hide and think, *That's crazy! God knows everything anyway.* It's easy to pass judgment on the first couple, but we do the same thing they did. This explains why the phobic person withdraws and hides and never resolves his problems.

I remember my own childish attempt at camouflaging my need for love. In grade school, whenever a certain boy teased me, I would blush furiously. I adored him, but I didn't want anyone to know my true feelings—least of all him!

The other students in my grade school teased me about the boy. I remember denying their accusations—I was ashamed of my feelings—and I didn't want anyone to know how I felt. I chose to hide my feelings, but everyone already knew the truth.

As I got older, the scenario repeated time and time again. Whenever I cared for a man, I inevitably blushed when I saw him. My friends said my face lit up like a neon sign whenever my current heartthrob entered the room.

I had great difficulty when the first man I cared deeply about told me he loved me. I loved him too, but I was afraid to respond to him. I lived in absolute terror of exposing my heart. Every time I came close to telling him how I felt, I would manufacture another excuse. I told myself I didn't need love, that I was too busy for this relationship, that my needs weren't that important anyway. Also, my farming background coupled with my Scandinavian stubbornness had planted in me an independent streak, and I feared that if I became vulnerable and admitted I needed him he would reject me.

A friend told me I was playing games and that I would be hurt. One day, Mother was standing in the room where I was talking to this man on the phone. "This has gone on long enough," she scolded. "If you won't tell him, I will. It's time he knows the truth."

She was kind enough to not make good on her threat, and I continued to hide my feelings from him for a long time. He got very frustrated with me, and by the time I was finally able to tell him how I felt, he had found someone else. I lost a significant relationship with a man I really cared about because I would not be honest about my feelings and needs.

You may find yourself playing games to mask your feelings as I did. My pride and insecurity prevented me from receiving the love I yearned for. Since then, I have sought to connect with others on the basis of love and truth, and have been rewarded with several deep and fulfilling relationships.

As you begin to connect with others, build your relationships on the foundation of love and truth. Stop playing games and hiding your pain behind excuses. True power to construct new relationships comes when you open your heart to love.

The apostle John declared that God is light and that those who walk in light have fellowship with one another (1 John 1:7). He goes on to say, "Whoever claims to live in him [God] must walk as Jesus did" (1 John 2:6).

Jesus did not avoid relationship but sought it out. He drew the disciples to himself and spent intense time getting to know them and teaching them. Relationships were important to him, and he demonstrated that by the way he placed a priority on people in need. Following his example, the early church met in one another's homes and encouraged each other.

When we are hurt today, we do the opposite. We tend to isolate and withdraw from others. This process only increases anxiety. If you don't acknowledge your need to be loved and supported, you can withdraw and become reclusive. In extreme cases, the withdrawal is total and results in living in isolation in a "self-sufficient" lifestyle. To become a recluse out of fear flies in the face of Jesus' truths.

To become a recluse out of fear flies in the face of these truths. To associate, work, and socialize with others of like faith builds up the body of Christ. When Paul writes to the Thessalonians, the desire of his heart for them is clear: "May the Lord make your love increase and overflow for each other and for everyone else, just as ours does for you" (1 Thessalonians 3:12). He encourages us to acknowledge that we do need each other.

To heal from an anxiety disorder, you must allow others to comfort, support, care for, and reassure you. As you grow to trust them, your trust in God will also expand.

Confiding, supporting, loving—all are necessary ingredients for restoration and healthy living. We do need others to encourage, comfort, and urge us to live lives worthy of God.

Power Tools

Power Padlock: I'm a strong, independent person; I don't need people to love me.

Power Principle: God designed me to need others.

Power Passage: "The LORD God said, 'It is not good for the man to be alone. I will make a helper suitable for him'" (Genesis 2:18).

Power Question: Make a list of people whom you will let love you this week.

Power Padlock: My needs and desires aren't as important as yours; my needs don't matter.

Power Principle: My needs and desires do matter.

Power Passage: "Two are better than one, because they have a good return for their work: If one falls down, his friend can help him up. But pity the man who falls and has no one to help him up!" (Ecclesiastes 4:9–10).

Power Question: When you have problems or difficulties in your life, who will you let pick you up?

Power Padlock: I grew up in a good family; I never doubted I was loved.

Power Principle: My need for love will continue throughout my life.

Power Passage: "Live a life of love, just as Christ loved us and gave himself up for us" (Ephesians 5:2).

Power Question: Why do I resist letting others love me?

Power Padlock: I've got responsibilities with my family; I don't have time to spend with you.

Power Principle: Taking care of myself enables me better to care for my family and others.

Power Passage: "The LORD will guide you always; he will satisfy your needs in a sun-scorched land and will strengthen your frame. You will be like a well-watered garden, like a spring whose waters never fail" (Isaiah 58:11).

Power Question: Why do I tend to take care of others and not take care of myself?

Power Padlock: I have plenty of people who love me; I don't need you.

Power Principle: I can never have too many good people to love me.

Power Passage: "Carry each other's burdens, and in this way you will fulfill the law of Christ" (Galatians 6:2).

Power Question: How can I expand my pool of good people who can love me when I have needs?

Posttraumatic Stress Disorder Self-Discovery Tool

Directions: Please answer "yes" or "no" to each of these questions. (The results of this self-discovery are for information purposes only. Please see a mental-health professional for diagnosis and treatment.)

1. Have you experienced a rape, sexual or physical abuse, war, severe accident, natural disaster, or violent crime? Yes___ No___

2. Has your experience left you feeling intense terror, fear, or hopelessness? Yes___ No___

3. Do you relive the event via flashbacks, nightmares, or dreams? Yes___ No___

4. Do you attempt to avoid these flashbacks, memories or nightmares? Yes___ No___

5. Do you feel emotionally "numb" or disconnected more often than you feel connected? Yes___ No___

6. Do you have a nagging sense that something is wrong with you more than not, and do you feel you are "going crazy"? Yes___ No___

7. Are you easily startled or frightened by scents or sounds that bring back the past? Yes___ No___

8. Have you experienced these symptoms for at least three months after the original trauma? Yes___ No___

9. Do you have problems in your family, work, or social network because of your fear? Yes___ No___

If you answered yes to any of these questions, there is hope and help for you. Read on for more information on Posttraumatic Stress Disorder.

5 Posttraumatic Stress Disorder:
When Trauma Causes Your Mind to Split

What's that smell? Mike wonders as he walks briskly from the downtown parking garage toward the office building where he has an appointment. He's never been in this area of downtown before, but there is something familiar about the sounds and smells—*I know I've smelled that before.*

His curiosity peaked, Mike pauses before a shop door, leaning forward a bit to take a second sniff. His senses identify the bitter aroma as a mix of freshly ground ginger, curry, and soy sauce—an aroma familiar to him from his tour as a Navy pilot in Vietnam.

Without warning, the distinct scent unleashes a flood of memories. Usually he is able to avoid these triggers, but the unfamiliar territory had caught him off guard. His body begins to tingle, his heart races, and beads of perspiration pop up on his forehead. Instantly transported to the past, an out-of-body sensation takes over. Mike is powerless to stop the action-packed movie that unfolds, scene by scene, in his mind. He's back in Nam.

Mike knows the script by heart. His squadron is ordered to run a secret bombing raid that Mike's commander says will end the war. But as they near their target, they discover their mission is no secret to the enemy. As they fly near the target, a fierce and well-planned counterattack from the ground is launched. Smoke and debris fill the sky as one by one each plane in his squadron goes down in flames.

Tink! Tink! Tink! Tink! Tink

From his seat in the cockpit, Mike recognizes the sound of machine-gun fire ripping into the plane's fuselage. Another round of automatic fire tears into the tail and he feels the loss of control in the rudder. Another round finds its mark, and Mike knows the aircraft is doomed. He radios his position and that he is going down and holds the plane steady until his buddy, Randy, can clear the plane. Mike's eyes follow a chute down until he sees his friend land a few hundred yards from the riverbank. Without taking time to even whisper a prayer, Mike pulls the lever that propels him from the plane. Later he remembers with irony his only thought at that moment *"what goes up must come down."* How true! Mike himself is drifting down when a loud "BOOM" and a burst of flame signals his plane has hit the ground.

Mike's internal movie fragments when his feet hit the ground; the screen goes dark. He has tried many times to remember what happened after he landed, but he can only recall the intense humidity and wilting heat. In his mind, the movie resumes with the thunk-thunk-thunk of blades cutting through air as the rescue helicopter approaches. How Mike got to the riverbed remains a mystery. But here he is, along with his best buddy, Randy. They are bloody but alive.

The helicopter pilot lowers a rescue cable a couple hundred feet away. Mike shoves Randy forward—willing him to the cable and up to safety. As Randy grabs the cable and is hoisted up shots ring out from the trees on the opposite bank. One after another, the shots find their mark. Mike focuses on the look of shock on Randy's face, unable to look at the dozens of holes in his friend's chest. Here Mike's mental movie goes to single-frame action as Randy's grip on the cable fails and he plummets down, hitting the ground with a sickening thud.

Frozen with fear and overcome with a sense of utter helplessness, Mike crouches in the underbrush. For the first time he realizes that he might not make it. Randy is already gone but that is beyond Mike's comprehension at the moment. The sound of gunfire and a shouting voice urges him to grab the cable. As soon as he is hoisted on board, the chopper banks sharply and hastens away. And all Mike can think about is how to tell Randy's wife and two kids that he's not coming home.

In the end, Mike survives his tour in Vietnam. But his friend Randy isn't the only casualty on the riverbank that day. Where once faith and peace of mind had lived, tormenting questions take up residence in Mike's mind. *How did the enemy find out about our mission? What happened when I hit the ground? Why did I send Randy to the cable first? What was the point of this war after all?* He craves answers that will give meaning to his suffering. In their absence, Mike turns his rage toward God. *Where were you when the enemy attacked? Why did you let Randy die and leave his kids without a father? Why didn't you take me? What if I don't want to be alive?*

About six months after returning to the States, Mike's "movies" or flashbacks start. He's afraid to go to sleep because of the dreams. On those rare nights when he does nod off, the terrifying scene of his plane bursting into flames, the look on Randy's face, and the sound of enemy fire jerk him back to consciousness. He awakes to find himself wrapped in sheets twisted and sweaty from the war he has waged in his head. No matter how hard he tries he can't stop his mind from being overrun by these memories. This is a new war and the enemy—anxiety—invades his thoughts. Like a sniper, his memories lie hidden, attack without warning, then evade his conscious reasoning while waiting for the opportunity to attack again. *Why can't I control these memories? They open fire and I haven't even seen them coming! Maybe I'm cracking up!*

Despite Mike's invisible battles after the war, he gets married and develops a career. His leadership skills secure him a good position as a military consultant with an aerospace company. But as the frequency and intensity of the flashbacks increase, Mike experiences real difficulty concentrating. He confides in no one—he should be able to handle it. He doesn't want his wife to worry. He figures their friends at church will think he's crazy.

But now his job is on the line. That's why Mike is downtown today—he needs to keep this appointment or he may as well kiss his job goodbye. He recalls the latest confrontation with his boss: "Where is your head?" Mike's boss had demanded. "Physically you're here with me, but you are not really here. I watch you sometimes during meetings. You look like you're in a trance: your skin turns white, your pupils enlarge, and it becomes very clear that you're somewhere else."

Mike had felt his face turn red and his anger surge. He had gripped the back of his chair until his knuckles turned white. *This guy is such an idiot! How did he ever get into management? He's no leader—in Nam we had leaders, real men, men who died …* Mike thought. And then it hit him—*I don't want to live like this anymore.* With his fist tightening around the personnel evaluation his boss had given him, he took a deep breath to calm himself.

"I'm ashamed to admit it," Mike had acknowledged, "but you're right. I'm tired of pretending there's nothing wrong. It's about my time in Nam. I saw so many horrible things, and I just can't get them out of my head. I want to live in the present, but I can't."

"That's a tough problem, but lots of guys have dealt with this." Mike's boss was doing his best to be supportive. "You're a valuable employee, and I don't want to lose you, but you need to see a counselor, or I'm going to have to let you go."

Earlier that week, he had heard almost those same words from his wife. She had told him how more and more often he seemed frozen, emotionless, and without passion. Their marriage had been reduced to two people living parallel lives. Even though he loved her, he began to find ways to avoid any interaction with her. He couldn't tell her how guilty he felt to be the sole survivor of his squadron. She couldn't understand the loneliness. She would never know the kind of loss he felt—loss so deep he was unwilling to risk new friendships. As his feelings of guilt and abandonment had overtaken him, he began to hate the man he had become. His self-hatred led him to the conviction that he could not trust anyone else to love him either, including God.

With the flashbacks becoming more and more frequent, Mike started staying at the office or working out at the gym late into the night, coming home only to fall into bed exhausted. He feared he would loose his job, his wife, his mind—until one night his wife found him sitting and staring blankly at the den wall with a gun in his hand. That's when she had begged him to get help or she was leaving. She could not stand to see him in pain any longer.

With ultimatums from both his boss and his wife, Mike knew he was close to being found out. His camouflage of strength was about to be exposed. The military had trained him to believe that a soldier never quits, never gives up, and never shows weakness or fear. But he knew he could no longer hold it together internally, and his feelings of inadequacy and inferiority were getting nearer to the surface. He was ashamed and embarrassed at the thought of anyone even thinking he was less than 100 percent male. He had withdrawn from others so completely he had no one to talk to. He decided it was better to speak with a therapist—a stranger and a professional—than risk being exposed to anyone he knew personally.

So on this bright and sunny afternoon, Mike continued his dark walk down the street toward the counselor's office. *I'm never going to get better. There is nothing anyone can do to help me—I'm permanently messed up by the war—but I can't live like this any longer. The counselor will probably have me committed.* Desperate thoughts wash through his mind, replacing the nightmare memories. *I don't even know why I'm bothering with this visit. If there is a cure, wouldn't God have shown it to me by now? Well, at least I will be able to say I did my duty to my wife and boss.*

Determined to keep his word, Mike resolutely walks into the building, takes the elevator upward and enters the therapist's office.

After nearly an hour of answering the counselor's questions, Mike is surprised when Debbie indicates that she has completed her evaluation. First she congratulates him for coming in, since only a trained therapist could accurately diagnose his disorder. She explains that the group of all his symptoms point to an anxiety disorder called Posttraumatic Stress Disorder or PTSD. Mike doesn't know if he feels shame or relief when he hears his diagnosis. He is surprised that there is a name for his problem, and that the therapist understands what he'd been going through. For the first time in a long time he thinks, *maybe there is hope for me.* Facing his counselor, he asks "What is Posttraumatic Stress Disorder?"

What Is Posttraumatic Stress Disorder or PTSD?

The *Diagnostic and Statistical Manual of Mental Disorders* (*DSM-IV*) states, "The essential feature of Posttraumatic Stress Disorder is the development of characteristic symptoms following exposure to an extreme traumatic stress or involving direct personal experience of an event that involves actual or threatened death or serious injury, or other threat to one's physical integrity; or witnessing an event that involves death, injury, or a threat to the physical integrity of another person; or learning about unexpected or violent death, serious harm, or threat of death or injury experienced by a family member or other close associate. The person's response to the event must involve intense fear, helplessness, or horror."[1]

The traumatic event leaves an indelible impression. It haunts a person's body, mind, and spirit with recurrent memory experiences that involve all five senses. To stop these painful sensations, people with PTSD will avoid activities and social functions that may heighten memories of the trauma.

Where Do the Vivid Flashbacks and Violent Dreams Come From?

A significant symptom of PTSD is sharpened physical senses. The traumatic flashbacks or dreams can be triggered by all five: sight, smell, sound, taste, and touch. For example, a small child who saw her parent die in a car accident might remember the blood at the scene. A woman who was beaten or raped often recalls the body odor of her abuser. She begins to shake when her body "remembers." A high school student remembers the pop of the gun that killed his classmate. A woman shrinks from the touch of her new husband as she recalls the unwelcome advances of her father.

The original trauma can also trigger physical sensations that don't make sense and can't be accounted for. Often people with this and other anxiety disorders will see a doctor, seeking relief from their unexplainable symptoms.

The mind is also impacted by the event and sees a series of disjointed memory fragments. For example, someone might see repeated pictures of a street, but he might never be able to see the sequence of events that transpired during a robbery or violent crime. These intrusive thoughts or images do not form a complete picture by themselves.

The traumatic memories can encase individuals in a dark emotional tomb that progressively seals off every significant relationship. They try to escape, but can't. They want to be resurrected to a new life or at least to resume the life they had before the trauma—a life of connecting with others in healthy relationship.

It has been many years since Mike served in Vietnam. But the history of his past was triggered by the scent of Vietnamese food lingering in the air. He feels powerless to stop the flashbacks—his emotions are frozen in time—he can't establish new relationships—he can't concentrate long enough to keep a job—and he's tried to stop the memories from bombarding his fragile mind—but can't.

This flood of emotional pain has caused many diagnosed with PTSD to be frozen in the heart. I've counseled some spouses of Vietnam veterans who've complained about their spouse's inability to experience passion. A husband whose wife has been violated by sexual abuse, rape, or violence may see similar traits in his spouse. He feels frustrated because he can't do anything to eliminate these recurrent images from his loved one's mind. Even the loving touch of a spouse cannot thaw the dark heart frozen in time.

People with Posttraumatic Stress Disorder feel afraid and stuck in the past. They try to avoid the flood of intrusive memories, but they can't. They are angry at being forced to live in the past and they don't have the freedom to live in the present. If this describes you, take heart. You are not alone. Much more is known today about what triggers PTSD, and much more is known about effective treatment of PTSD in general.

How Common Is PTSD?

"As many as 70 percent of adults in the United States have experienced at least one major trauma in their lives, many of which have suffered from the emotional reactions that are called PTSD. It is estimated that 5 percent of the population currently have PTSD [and] that 8 percent have PTSD at some point in their lives."[2]

While women are twice as likely as men to have Posttraumatic Stress Disorder, it is highly probable that men do not report PTSD. Men are more likely to cover their pain with substance abuse and sexual addiction.

For women, the most common events that trigger the disorder are rape, sexual molestation, physical attack, being threatened with a weapon, and childhood physical abuse. Men are more likely to experience trauma relating to physical abuse, violent crime, and war.

The Surgeon General explains there is a connection between Posttraumatic Stress Disorder and the military. "Thirty percent of men and women who have spent time in war zones experience PTSD."[3] That means that almost one in three of the men and women in the armed forces have a possibility of experiencing PTSD.

Among Vietnam veterans the number of soldiers diagnosed with Posttraumatic Stress Disorder is staggering. A government survey found these numbers soar to about 1,700,000 veterans who experienced "clinically serious stress reaction symptoms."[4] Studies further uncovered some of the serious consequences of PTSD.

- 40% of Vietnam veteran men have been divorced at least once
- 23% have high levels of parenting problems
- Almost 50% of male veterans have been arrested or jailed at least once
- 11% have been convicted of a felony
- 39% abuse or are dependent on alcohol
- 11% of veteran's children are alcohol dependent or abusers

Sexual addiction, relational problems, depression, and a host of other mental disorders accompany Posttraumatic Stress Disorder. In addition, people with PTSD often suffer from survivor's guilt. Some soldiers experience guilt during the war because they lived and another died. A victim of the 9/11 disaster might hold himself responsible for making it out of the building or not going to work that day. And a rape victim may blame herself for walking alone to her car late at night. For these people, the world becomes increasingly disjointed and disconnected.

If you feel this way, you would benefit from professional and compassionate therapy.

Why Is Substance Abuse Connected with PTSD?

An increasing number of patients are developing dual diagnoses—problems with both substance abuse and PTSD. Estimates now suggest that sixty to eighty percent of those people diagnosed with Posttraumatic Stress Disorder have a substance abuse problem. On the other hand, only forty to sixty percent of all people with substance abuse issues have PTSD as a primary diagnosis. Experts say this difference reflects that PTSD is "under-diagnosed" by health care professionals and may occur more frequently than figures indicate.

There are three major theories about how substance abuse and Posttraumatic Stress Disorder are connected. First, substance abuse is a means of avoiding or denying the "re-experiencing" of the painful trauma. Alcohol and other drugs are used to numb the pain. A second theory explains that alcoholism develops first and sets the stage for the development of PTSD in the future. A third theory says that substance abuse becomes a form of self-medication for the symptoms of PTSD. Alcohol and other drugs are used to help a person sleep, reduce depression and anxiety, and avoid painful issues. Initial studies indicate that substance abuse becomes a problem for more chronic, long-term cases where hopelessness and despair begin to develop.

Who Are the Candidates for Posttraumatic Stress Disorder?

Early research on the topic of trauma began during the late 1800s as trains carried passengers across the new frontier. When the primitive trains derailed, people were seriously injured—some were left permanently disabled. Experts discovered the victims of these accidents had recurring flashbacks of the horrific scenes. Extended family members sued the railroad companies and won. These corporations funded some of the early studies on PTSD, which eventually led researchers back as far as the Revolutionary and Civil Wars.

Early in the twentieth century, research on PTSD continued following World Wars I and II. "Shellshock" was the term used to describe the impact of trauma on soldiers. Many indicated that it was impossible to live a "normal life" following the war. The images of combat were forever branded in their minds.

In the years following World War II, additional research first connected PTSD to concentration camp survivors. Later, a significant connection was made with PTSD to the intense pain of sexual, physical, and emotional abuse. Further research also uncovered a link between natural disasters, accidents, and violent crimes. There are many others who've been held hostage, kidnapped, or held at gunpoint and develop PTSD. Some children who've had extended hospital stays endure PTSD as a result of separation from their families. The results on the victims are devastating. For example, as many as 50 percent of rape victims report suicidal feelings—they simply can't cope with the pain created by the crime. There are even documented accounts of missionaries who were raped, held hostage at gunpoint, or tortured for their faith and who were later diagnosed with Posttraumatic Stress Disorder.[5]

Further study into the field of PTSD now includes the affects on those who work closely with the victims of trauma including missionaries, pastors, counselors, healthcare workers, and others. Second-hand trauma—dealing with those who have experienced trauma and feeling a responsibility to help—is also being shown to have devastating repercussions.

However overwhelming your feelings of helplessness and hopelessness have become, the temptation is to believe there isn't any hope. I've seen the lives of many broken clients who've experienced violent sexual and physical abuse, horrific scenes of war, and life-endangering accidents reach out to God and others to recover from PTSD.

What Are the Symptoms for Posttraumatic Stress Disorder?

- Decreased self-esteem from an inability to get or keep a job

- Loss of sustained beliefs about people and society following the trauma
- Hopelessness that the flashbacks and dreams will stop
- A sense of being permanently damaged with no hope for recovery
- Difficulties with maintaining previously established relationships

What Is the Difference between Acute Stress and PTSD?

If these symptoms emerged within a month of the trauma, they are considered Acute Stress. With PTSD, the symptoms continue for a period longer than six months and don't begin for at least three months following the trauma.[6]

There are three types of Posttraumatic Stress disorder:[7]

- Acute (Stress), lasting less than three months
- Chronic, lasting more than three months
- Delayed, beginning at least 6 months after exposure to the trauma

According to the Surgeon General, "About 50 percent of cases of Posttraumatic stress disorder remit within 6 months. For the remainder, the disorder typically persists for years and can dominate the sufferer's life."[8] Many people diagnosed with PTSD, as well as those suffering from other anxiety disorders, feel they're going crazy. They are tormented by the frequent dreams and flashbacks and are unable to cope with the anxiety.

How Does Disassociation Differ from Other Types of Pain?

People can experience trauma in different ways—through war, crime, abuse, and other catastrophic events. For all of these injuries there are generally three main categories of response. The following tree metaphors may help you understand these categories more clearly:

Healthy Recovery. A beautiful fir tree stands straight and tall, its branches filled with vibrant green needles. It has weathered many storms and sports a few scars on its tall trunk. If you could examine its rings in the core of its trunk, you would see it has lived through drought and fire. But it has learned to thrive in its environment and is well on its way to becoming a giant. The growing fir tree represents a healthy person developing without dysfunction in spite of the trauma.

Stunted Growth. Another fir tree is not fairing as well. It is a struggling seedling that appears to be losing its needles, a sign it is dying from some internal malady. Virtually undetectable from the outside, an insect has found its way inside the protective bark and is slowly eating away the core of the tree. This tree will die slowly from the inside out—a victim of its environment. The struggling sapling reminds me of people who grow up in homes where they have experienced severe abuse, alcoholism, or extreme chaos.

> "Even though I walk through the valley of the shadow of death, I will fear no evil, for you are with me; your rod and your staff, they comfort me" (Psalm 23:4).

Survivor's Denial. A third tree has been struck by lightning. The impact of the storm almost split the tree in two—a section of the trunk has broken away. The tree did nothing to produce the lightning; it was an accident. The tree was not at fault; it could do nothing to prevent the sudden strike. The tree is trying to live on despite the brokenness in its trunk. It will take time for the tree to realize that it needs a whole trunk to function as it was designed to function. If the tree were a person, it might try to bury the broken part of the trunk and live as if it didn't exist. We call this disassociation. What the traumatized tree (and the person) really needs is to acknowledge the wound and bind up the brokenness. Healing comes when the buried part is integrated again into the rest of the tree.

When people experience this kind of deep emotional trauma, their minds can't comprehend what their eyes are seeing. The mind attempts to stabilize by "splitting off." This complicated process—called "disassociation"—may be a conscious or unconscious process used by the mind to organize and balance in the face of a frightening, overwhelming, disorganized event.

I remember hearing a story about a woman who coped with childhood sexual abuse by disassociating. One autumn day, she was raped under a walnut tree. Her mind couldn't process what was happening to her, so she focused on a single leaf turning color above her. In an effort to stabilize, her mind chose to look at what was happening from the view of the leaf. She watched from above, seeing the man who was violating her. She could do nothing to save herself.

I also remember visiting the Holocaust Museum in Israel. The drawings made by children in the concentration camps left a lasting impression on me. The pictures included scenes of bright flowers in a field. The children's minds had fixed on an image far from the contrasting reality of smelters sending plumes of black smoke from burning bodies across the countryside.

Victims of traumatic experiences will often focus on the color of the wall, the dish on the nightstand, or the scent of the room. They tend to focus on these seemingly insignificant items to distract from the pain of the event.

When my patients who have Posttraumatic Stress disorder begin to disassociate, they go into a shock-like physical state: their faces turn white—their pupils enlarge—and they lose touch with the world around them. They appear to have seen something startling, and they disconnect from reality. At these times I encourage them to breathe and relax while I pat their face, rub their hands, or ask for touch from others to help them reconnect with the here and now. Physical contact and human touch can help them organize thoughts, feelings, and experiences and bring them back to the present where hope and healing can be found.

How Do Love and Limits Build Healthy Relationships?

Many people with PTSD experienced a violation of their personal boundaries through a traumatic event. For example, a young boy's boundaries are crossed when his mother beats him. An accident or traumatic event can disorganize a person's trust and lead him to hold the world around him as unsafe and unstable. The Holocaust survivors' boundaries were crossed in many ways. Research on Holocaust survivors and other victims of trauma indicates that healing comes as people enter into relationship with those who are safe and have good boundaries.

Every day is a new day. We need to allow others to help us make a fresh start.

Why Do Limits Demonstrate Love?

Before I became a therapist, I was a youth worker for over twenty years. For ten years, I directed a national youth organization that ministered to students on public junior high, high school, and college campuses across the country.

On one local campus, my staff and I developed a ministry to cheerleaders, student athletes, and student leaders. One of my concerns for this group of students was that they were selfish and lacked empathy. They were unaware of the needs of others.

My goal with these students was to teach them to open their eyes and hearts and to love others who were not as fortunate as they were. We organized many activities to bring these students into contact with others in need. We traveled to an inner-city mission to serve Thanksgiving dinner to the homeless. At Christmas, I took them to a home where severely challenged children lived. We sang Christmas carols to patients whose families had abandoned them—these patients would have no holiday visitors. On Easter Sunday, we conducted a church service in a nursing home.

The students performed well and had earned a celebration. One summer's day we packed up loads of goodies donated by a local grocery store manager and set off to feast and frolic at a nearby park. We were having a great time grilling hamburgers and hotdogs, when some children with physical and emotional challenges entered the area. As these children attempted to play baseball, students in our group began to make fun of them. There was obviously no way these children could begin to compete with the school's star player, a member of our group, proudly dressed in his letterman's jacket as a testament to his athletic achievements.

I wasted no time gathering together the high school students, letting them know how unacceptable their behavior was. We went on to quickly finish our meal and were in the midst of roasting marshmallows when a few of the guys again started criticizing the children's athletic abilities.

I felt my anger swell, and my patience was nearly gone. I again made it clear that this behavior was unacceptable. This time I added that the consequence of it continuing would be the end of our picnic. We would pack up and go home. The students made the choice to continue the teasing and I had no choice but to stand by the limits I had set for them. Over their protests, I told them to pack up their things and get on the bus. I'll never forget the ride home. Imagine a bus full of silent teenagers. No one dared to say a word. Twenty minutes never lasted so long!

The next evening we'd planned a special outreach event for students from area schools. We had a special speaker coming to our center with music, games, and activities. I tossed and turned that night, wondering how my actions from the day might affect the turnout for the coming event.

When the night of the big event arrived, much to my surprise, students filled the auditorium. There were more teens than we'd ever had at any previous event. At the reception afterward, my curiosity peaked and I approached the student I'd been so tough with the day before.

"I'm curious," I said with a puzzled tone. "Why do you think so many kids turned out for this event?

The student didn't respond.

"Was it the great music?"

The student leader shook his head.

"Was it the famous athlete who spoke?" I continued.

"You just don't get it, do you?" He looked straight into my eyes and continued with the words I still clearly remember. "It's because you set limits with us."

"What do you mean?" I asked the star athlete.

"Yesterday you cared enough about us to say no to us. We all got to talking at school today, and we knew what we did at the park was wrong." He paused before he added, "And we wished our parents loved us enough to say no."

I was astounded. Here I was worrying that by being tough I had alienated these students but he was standing there telling me the opposite was true. I knew the story of his tattered childhood and his painful experience with his parents' divorce. I wasn't a therapist at that point, but I learned an important lesson that day—one I've often drawn upon in working with my patients.

Loving limits are a tool to show someone you care. People may say they don't want to be held accountable, but in actuality they need someone who has the courage to lovingly establish boundaries.

There is a clear difference between abusive limits and healthy boundaries. Abusive limits demand power and control. Healthy boundaries provide choices and options; they aren't demeaning and abrasive. They don't tell people what they must do, but they can be used to lovingly guide others toward truth. As a youth worker, I gave the teens choices and consequences regarding their behavior. I would have liked to stay at the park if the cruel teasing had stopped. In some ways it would have been easier too. But when the kids decided teasing was more important than the picnic, I had to set aside what I wanted and love them enough to enforce my stated consequences.

When we establish firm limits with love, we hold a dynamic power to heal the broken part of our hearts. People with Posttraumatic Stress Disorder need the structure of loving limits to take back control of their anxiety-ridden bodies and face their fears. They need reassurance and they need to be accountable in ways that allow them to overcome their anxious thoughts and choose to engage in loving relationships again.

In our minds, our fears are magnified. We allow the event that caused us so great a trauma to have power over us. Our inability to control our anxiety significantly diminishes our power to rise above our anxiety.

Jesus suffered in every way that a man can suffer. In the midst of his wilderness wanderings, after forty days of fasting, thirst, heat, and loneliness, Jesus faced down emotional pain by turning to the comfort and protection of God's own words. Do you know why his words held such power? Because they are the true promises of the Almighty and absolutely trustworthy.

You may want to try "praying the Scriptures" on your own behalf. Start with Isaiah 45:2: "I will go before you and will level the mountains; I will break down gates of bronze and cut through bars of iron." God's omnipotent power can slice through whatever strongholds bind you, no matter how strong the strongholds!

Do you sometimes feel overpowered by your anxiety? The emotional pain and fear is your wilderness. But like Jesus, you don't have to remain there. The great news is that while you may *feel* alone in your pain, you are *never* abandoned. Listen to God's loving words for you: "Because of the LORD's great love we are not consumed, for his compassions never fail" (Lamentations 3:22).

What an amazing truth! As fearful and outnumbered as you think you are, this is your great hope. And it only gets better. Hear how God responds when his people are under attack: "In all their distress he too was distressed, and the angel of his presence saved them. In his love and mercy he redeemed them; he lifted them up and carried them all the days of old" (Isaiah 63:9).

God wants to carry you up and out of your distress. He will prevent you from being consumed by your past. Let him enable you to begin the healing.

Power Tools for Empowered Living

Finding freedom from the past is difficult. We often harbor beliefs about ourselves that inhibit healing. These beliefs are usually based on untruths. God's truth is the key to unlocking the "Power Padlocks" that keep us from finding freedom from fear.

For every Power Padlock there is a Power Principle or scriptural truth to counteract the lie. These scriptural truths are supported by the Bible verses listed in the Power Passage. Together they help you discover a way to apply the truth to your life. Check out the Power Tools for Posttraumatic Stress Disorder below.

Power Padlock: People who set limits on me don't understand or care about me.

Power Principle: True love means setting limits and sometimes saying no.

Power Passage: "No discipline seems pleasant at the time, but painful. Later on, however, it produces a harvest of righteousness and peace for those who have been trained by it" (Hebrews 12:11).

Power Question: How do I feel inside when People say no to me or when I try to control them?

Power Padlock: If I tell someone how I really feel they will reject me.

Power Principle: True love means I can be honest with others about my feelings.

Power Passage: "Instead, speaking the truth in love, we will in all things grow up into him who is the Head, that is, Christ. From him the whole body, joined and held together by every supporting ligament, grows and builds itself up in love, as each part does its work" (Ephesians 4:15–16).

Power Question: How do I feel on the inside when others give me constructive criticism or tell me something I don't want to hear about myself?

Power Padlock: I'm afraid if I love someone, they will have too much control over me.

Power Principle: True love means being in relationship with others in order to grow.

Power Passage: "There is no fear in love. But perfect love drives out fear, because fear has to do with punishment. The one who fears is not made perfect in love" (1 John 4:18).

Power Question: How can I establish limits so others don't control me and I have the freedom to love?

Power Padlock: My past will always limit my ability to love.

Power Principle: God will redeem my past and empower my present and future.

Power Passage: "This is what the LORD says ... Forget the former things; do not dwell on the past. See, I am doing a new thing! Now it springs up; do you not perceive it? I am making a way in the desert and streams in the wasteland" (Isaiah 43:16, 18–19).

Power Question: How can God use my past to prepare me for the future?

Self-Discovery on Panic

Directions: Please answer "yes" or "no" to each of these questions. (The results of this self-discovery are for information purposes only. Please see a mental-health professional for diagnosis and treatment.)

1. Does your heart ever seem to skip a beat or do you find yourself gasping for breath? Yes____ No____

2. Have you felt like you're choking when you're not? Yes____ No____

3. Have you ever woken from your sleep to find you're having another of these "attacks?" Yes____ No____

4. Did your heart pound or race during these attacks? Yes____ No____

5. Do you to feel out of control and helpless when you have these attacks? Yes____ No____

6. When you're afraid, do you feel an intense tingling sensation in your toes or hands or on your skin? Yes____ No____

7. Did the physical sensation or attacks subside in 5 – 30 minutes after onset? Yes____ No____

8. Were there chills or hot flashes that accompanied your attack? Yes____ No____

9. Have you been diagnosed with another anxiety disorder or depression? Yes____ No____

10. Do you remember any of these attacks emerging during your childhood? Yes____ No____

If you've experienced the above symptoms, have you …

11. Feared traveling or getting caught in a crowd if you have another attack? Yes____ No____

12. Changed your life to avoid the attacks? Yes____ No____

13. Had blurred or tunnel vision, making it difficult to see? Yes____ No____

14. Avoided certain events or objects because you fear you will have another episode? Yes____ No____

If you answered, "yes" to any of these questions, read on to find out more about Panic Disorder.

6 Panic Disorder:
When It Feels Like Your Life Is Out of Control

I can't breathe. Paula feels her throat tighten as if an unseen assailant, his hands wrapped around her neck, is squeezing the breath from her. "I've got to get out of here! Something's wrong!" Paula tells her teenage son Josh as she feels a familiar knot forming in her stomach.

Paula and Josh are in the grocery store to pick up a few last-minute items for Easter dinner when Paula suddenly feels shortness of breath followed by a tingling sensation running down her arm and into her chest. Soon nausea and stronger chest pains wash over her. Josh's face is white and his eyes wide as he watches his mom grimace in pain. He doesn't know what to do so he begins to scan the people in the store to find someone to help.

As her knees begin to buckle, she and Josh race from the store. She doesn't want to collapse in front of everyone.

I've got to stay calm, Paula tells herself even as she wonders, *Is this what a heart attack feels like? Is this what it feels like to die?*

I'm not going to make it, Paula tells herself as she flushes and sweat begins to run down her face. With Josh's help, Paula makes her way to their car. "Josh, I think you should take me to the emergency room—quickly," she pants as she eases into the passenger seat. Josh hurries around the car and slides in behind the wheel. Trying not to alarm her son further, Paula feels like she is choking with every shallow breath. The weight on her chest is crushing. She whispers a desperate prayer and rests her head gingerly on the back of the seat as Josh makes his way through traffic toward the hospital. He prays they will be in time.

Entering the ER, Paula's thoughts flash back several years to the last time she passed through those automatic doors. It was in this hospital ER her husband Jack had lost his battle with cancer. During the many months she had tenderly cared for him at home, he had faded into a mere shadow of the robust Norwegian track star she had married twenty years before. But that day as the ambulance pulled away from their home, she knew he would never return. Twelve-year-old Josh had stood in the driveway with his hand resting on the slim shoulder of his younger sister, Katie. Paula remembers watching from the rear window of the ambulance, hot tears making their way down her face. Katie was crying too. But not Josh—he stood strong and tall—determined to be the new man of the house and to take care of his sister and mom.

An orderly wheels Paula's gurney into the trauma center. Into the room rushes a team of healthcare professionals who immediately start working on her. One grabs a blood pressure cuff. Another hooks Paula up to a monitor. A third nurse inserts an IV and takes blood samples for the lab. While Josh paces anxiously in the waiting room, Paula is surrounded by strangers who poke and prod her in an effort to discover the cause of her pain.

Beep!

Beep!

Beep!

The monitor rhythmically keeps time with Paula's every heartbeat. On Paula's right the nurse taking her blood pressure readings visibly relaxes and the trauma team's pace slows as Paula's vital signs indicate she is stabilizing. An aid leaves the room to reassure Josh that his mother is going to be okay.

Within a short time, Paula feels the pains subside and so does the flurry of activity around her. As the medication takes affect and the stress of the moment eases, Paula realizes she is exhausted. She has started to doze when a middle-aged man dressed in a white shirt and tie enters the room, introducing himself as Dr. Barnes. After consulting her chart, he asks her a series of questions about medications, prior illnesses, and physical conditions, as well as the events leading up to her attack. Then suddenly the focus of his questioning seems to shift.

"Have you ever had similar pains before?" the doctor asks her. Paula glances around the room uncomfortably as she weighs her answer.

The last beat of Jack's heart five years ago marked a turning point for Paula. That day she fell into a spiral of grief and anger that lasted for many months. The harder she fought to find her way out, the deeper into despair she sank. She was a single mother now with children to nurture and provide for—but how? Each day's worries seemed to grow exponentially until she feared she would never manage on her own. At that time none of them thought they could survive the grief and fear of living without Jack. And Paula felt she'd rather die than go on alone.

"W-w-well," Paula stammers in reply to Dr. Barnes' questioning, "I guess I have."

"That's what I thought," the doctor comments. "Can you tell me more about them?"

Paula pauses for a moment and looks at the floor.

"I need you to be honest with me if I'm going to help you," the doctor prompts.

Reluctantly Paula recites her history of pain. "I had some pains as a child when my mother died. I felt abandoned because no one wanted me until my grandfather took me in. In my senior year of college, just before I married Jack, I had a few spells of chest pains and dizziness. I was having trouble concentrating in class too. When I went to the doctor and he found out I was getting married in a few weeks, he said it was only anxiety and sent me home. He must have been right because the pains subsided for almost twenty years—until my husband died. Since then I've had chest pains occasionally, and once I ended up in the ER—but those attacks were nothing like today."

Paula pauses and looks at the doctor for reassurance. After examining her further and consulting the results of her tests, the doctor is able to assure Paula that everything appears normal.

"There doesn't seem to be a problem with your heart," he concludes. He pauses for a moment to look at her chart. "Many people come to the ER thinking they are having a heart attack or choking, but they're actually having a panic attack."

"What do you mean, 'panic attack'?" Paula asks.

The doctor explains, "I mean you are experiencing a kind of anxiety known as panic."

"You mean I'm not going to die?" Paula questions.

"You're not going to die," he tells her with a smile. "At least not yet! You know it will happen to all of us at some time. But I've never heard of anyone dying from a panic attack. They're not fatal."

Paula takes a deep breath and gives a sigh of relief. Her mind drifts to the Easter dinner waiting at home. She can almost taste the honey-glazed ham, the baked sweet potatoes smothered in butter and sprinkled with brown sugar, and the hot yeast rolls fresh from the oven. She thanks God for his protection and smiles. A short while later she is discharged with written instructions about her medication and a referral to a licensed counselor to learn how to manage her anxiety issues. Paula walks into the waiting room, embraces her son and says, "Let's go eat."

After enjoying a wonderful Easter dinner with her family, Paula admits to her children for the first time just how overwhelmed she has sometimes felt in the past, especially in the years since Jack's death. She tells Josh and Katie about the doctor's recommendation that she see a therapist and they whole-heartedly support her. The next morning Paula calls and schedules an appointment later that week. True to her word, Katie drives her mother to the counselor's office and settles into a chair in the waiting room until the appointment is over.

After introducing herself with a handshake, Paula sits across from Debbie, the counselor, and listens as, for the first time, someone explains to her about her attacks and Panic Disorder.

What Is Panic Disorder?

According to the *Diagnostic and Statistical Manual of Mental Disorders* (*DSM-IV*), "The essential feature of Panic Disorder is the presence of recurrent, unexpected panic attacks followed by at least 1 month of persistent concern about having another panic attack, worry about the possible implications or consequences of the panic attacks, or a significant behavioral change related to the attacks."[1]

Panic can affect people at any age. Some research suggests it can peak during late adolescence and again in the mid-thirties. Some begin in childhood, but onset after age forty-five is rare. The earlier the onset of the disorder, the more difficulty a person is likely to experience. Studies in children with panic disorder have found ...

- 50% will develop agoraphobia
- 20% will make suicide attempts
- 27% will develop alcohol abuse
- 60% will develop depression
- 35% will believe they are unhealthy
- 27% will be financially dependent
- 28% will make frequent outpatient visits
- 50% will have significant social impairment.[2]

The roots of Paula's panic were uncovered with the doctor in the emergency room. They were traced to her childhood and emerged later in life. However, the attacks reappeared at various crisis points in her life as well: the death of her husband, loss of her job, and an accident on the freeway. Her fear of not being able to control the panic attacks increased her anxiety, making the possibility of an attack greater.

How Common Is Panic?

According to the National Institute of Mental Health, "About 1.7% of the adult US population ages 18 to 54—approximately 2.4 million Americans—has panic."[3]

Others have explained, "Panic Disorder is a serious condition that around one out of every 75 people might experience. It usually appears during the teens or early adulthood, and while the exact causes are unclear, there does seem to be a connection with major life transitions that are potentially stressful: graduating from college, getting married, having a first child, and so on."[4]

Some think there is a genetic predisposition for panic and other anxiety disorders. If one of your family members has panic disorder, you may have an increased risk of suffering from it yourself, but panic is hard to diagnose because so many people focus on the physical symptoms, believing something is wrong with their body.

"One study found that people sometimes see ten or more doctors before being properly diagnosed, and that only one out of four of people with the disorder receive the treatment they need."[5] Paula was fortunate in that she had an emergency room doctor who had seen panic before, and who didn't release her without further investigation into her past history.

What Are the Symptoms of Panic?

According to the *Diagnostic and Statistical Manual of Mental Disorders* (*DSM-IV*), panic is "a discrete period of intense fear or discomfort. ... The attack has a sudden onset and builds to a peak rapidly (usually in 10 minutes or less) and is often accompanied by a sense of imminent danger or impending doom and an urge to escape."[6] These are the symptoms:

- Palpitations, pounding heart, or accelerated heart rate
- Sweating
- Trembling or shaking
- Sensations of shortness of breath or smothering
- Feeling of choking
- Chest pain or discomfort
- Nausea or abdominal distress
- Feeling dizzy, unsteady, lightheaded, or faint
- Derealization (feelings of unreality) or depersonalization (being detached from one's self)
- Fear of losing control or going crazy

- Fear of dying
- Paralysis (numbing or tingling sensations)
- Chills or hot flashes[7]

What Are the Real Issues Behind Panic?

The real problem behind panic is the fear of having another attack and being out of control in public. People with panic disorder live with the realization that these attacks can occur at any time and any place. Unlike other anxiety disorders, it is not the fear of avoiding different situations or objects, such as snakes or spiders. It is the fear of the response to these objects or situations or another attack that causes the problems.

People with panic disorder fear the embarrassment of having another person observe them having an attack. This results in a pattern of avoidance of others that in the worst case can develop into agoraphobia (abnormal fear of embarrassment in public) or even a fear of everything (General Anxiety Disorder). People with panic begin to withdraw from relationships and develop intense feelings of loneliness and abandonment.

What Is the Relationship between Panic and Phobia?

People with panic attacks can be diagnosed with or without agoraphobia. They live in fear of having a panic attack in public and progressively withdraw from life.

In the chapter on specific phobia, we watched Sarah as she was diagnosed with agoraphobia. Often, but not always, that accompanies panic disorder. Paula and Sarah's cases are different. Sarah has a phobia of open spaces that has developed into an avoidance of all places except her house. Paula's panic has not yet escalated into agoraphobia because she can still go out in public.

Where Does Panic Disorder Come From?

Many clinicians feel that panic disorder has a strong biological/genetic link. Others think there is a strong connection between learning or conditioning problems and panic. People with panic are more sensitized and have a more intense response to life's difficulties. It is thought that the disorder is maintained by negative reinforcement and irrational thinking patterns. The Book of Proverbs affirms the relationship of our thoughts to our behavior when it says, "As a [person] thinks in his heart, so is he" (Proverbs 23:7, KJV).

Do Panic Attacks Always Signal a Mental Disorder?

According to the Surgeon General's report, "Panic attacks are not always indicative of a mental disorder, and up to 10 percent of otherwise healthy people experience an isolated panic attack per year."[8]

Until the 60s, panic attacks were not recognized as a separate diagnosis. At that time, healthcare providers started to differentiate between patients who had unexpected anxiety attacks and those with other anxiety disorders. Additional study created a separate diagnostic category for people with these severe physical symptoms.

Panic attacks are often confusing to diagnose because they can accompany many of the other disorders, including Social Phobia, Generalized Anxiety Disorder, and major depression. Expert examination is needed to tell the difference between Panic Disorder and panic attacks within these categories. To receive a primary diagnosis of Panic Disorder, there must be at least two documented cases of an attack and evidence of an attempt to avoid the physical symptoms mentioned above.

What Other Health Issues Confront People with Panic?

There is also a connection between panic and other health issues. People who suffer from panic disorder

- are more prone to alcohol and other drug abuse;
- have a greater risk for suicide;
- spend more time in hospital emergency rooms;
- tend to be financially dependent on others;
- are afraid of driving more than a few miles from home;
- and have a higher rate than the rest of the population of irritable bowel syndrome.

What Do People Diagnosed with Panic Need Most?

People diagnosed with panic, as well as other anxiety disorders, need love, encouragement, and accountability. They need to know if they do or do not have an attack, they are still good, worthwhile people. When they have a panic attack, they feel they're "bad." If they were "good," they would be able to control their lives. They feel a sense of public humiliation when their weakness is not controlled but exposed.

People with panic attacks have huge problems with what psychologists call "splitting." They see their disorder as bad and unacceptable. They try to deny their fear and present a front of self-confidence.

As children, they do not develop a sense of self-control and boundaries in their thinking and behavior. For example, when an eight-year-old is told he is bad because he spilled his milk, he comes to believe that he as a person is bad, rather than understanding that he simply made a mistake. The child needs the parent to love him despite his failures, in other words, to love him unconditionally. Part of this love is encouraging him to change his behavior by allowing him to take responsibility for his actions. The eight-year-old who spills can clean up the mess.

Part of growing up is reconciling the good parts with the bad parts. We learn to accept strength and weakness in ourselves. People with panic attacks have difficulty in accepting the good part of them. Love helps us to see our "bad" and accept it.

Remember how God sees you. After all, he made you and knows you better than you know yourself. Listen to how loving and personal he gets with his people, Israel (Jacob): "But now, this is what the LORD says—he who created you, O Jacob, he who formed you, O Israel: 'Fear not, for I have redeemed you; I have called you by name; you are mine'" (Isaiah 43:1).

How Do We Expose Our Pain?

When I was a child, I learned an important lesson about love and acceptance.

My life in the country was typical. We lived in a white farmhouse built around 1900. It had four steps leading to a big porch. Ornately carved pillars lined the porch, enhancing its beauty and charm.

One day Mother and I were returning from shopping when I spotted red blood splattered on the white steps. When I saw my pet collie, Susie, standing at the top of the steps—my heart skipped a beat and I became hysterical.

"She is bleeding! She is dying!" I yelled to mother in a panic. "We've got to take Suzie to the emergency room."

Mother turned her face from me, using her hands to shield her gentle smile. I learned several years later that she hadn't wanted to embarrass or laugh at her innocent daughter.

When she regained her composure, she said, "I think it is time we have a talk about the birds and the bees. ..." That day I received my first of many farm sex education lessons from Mother. These lessons continued while I watched the birth and death of our farm animals.

Near the end of Suzie's life, I was privileged to be there when she had her last litter of puppies. I was thrilled watching the birth process. We were all in awe as she panted. Silence followed the birth of the last brownish colored pup. Suddenly I heard a noise and saw two more tiny back legs emerging—a thirteenth puppy was being born breach. I panicked when I realized this last one had only three legs. My heart pounded. How can this dog possibly have a normal life? How will he walk and play like a normal dog?

I was worried about my three-legged friend when I was at school. Each day, I raced from the school bus to be with my special puppy. Suzie and I worked with little "Half-pint" to help him learn to walk. I was determined that I would find a way. There was no doubt about it: "Half-pint" won his way into my heart.

> "Praise be to the God and Father of our Lord Jesus Christ, the Father of compassion and the God of all comfort, who comforts us in all our troubles, so that we can comfort those in any trouble with the comfort we ourselves have received from God" (2 Corinthians 2:3).

All my efforts paid off. The day finally came when I saw my three-legged friend walk. I was so proud that I told my friends at school about my accomplishments. My teacher overheard me talking about Half-pint and without my knowledge went to the office and telephoned my mom. She asked Mother to bring my puppy to class to illustrate a unit she was teaching us about physical and mental disabilities.

Mother brought Half-pint to school to show the students and then to a courtyard below the classroom where we could all watch this three-legged dog walk. He walked easily on even pavement, but had difficulty on gravel. My three-legged puppy dog became the talk of my sixth-grade class.

A father of one of my classmates was a television newsperson. That night my friend told her father about my dog. He called my mother and asked if he could film the story. It was shown on the Seattle television station and continued on to several other networks. The television station received letters from across the country because of this now-famous three-legged puppy dog.

From my childhood experience, I learned an important lesson about exposing "bad." My dog's deformity didn't make her bad or any less of a dog, rather it helped to make her special. When we can bring our "bad" into healthy relationship, God can use it to comfort and encourage others.

Sometimes our problems seem pointless and overwhelming. But we know that along with our troubles, God brings comfort. We must understand that being comforted can also mean receiving strength, encouragement, and hope to deal with our troubles. If you are feeling overwhelmed, allow God to comfort you.

Jesus said, "Blessed are those who mourn, for they will be comforted" (Matthew 5:4). Mourning, in this context, means we bring our bad into relationship. Many of us limit our mourning to prayer and other "spiritual" activities, but comfort comes when we open our whole selves—good and bad—to relationships based on love and limits. If you're feeling overwhelmed, you must learn to ask for and seek comfort from God and others. In doing so, you will experience God's supernatural power to accept yourself just as you are.

He is personally interested in each one of us: "For I am the LORD, your God, who takes hold of your right hand and says to you, Do not fear; I will help you" (Isaiah 41:13).

A panic-bound life is not the abundant life that God intends for us. He wants for us what Paul prayed for the Ephesians: "I pray that out of his glorious riches he may strengthen you with power through his Spirit in your inner being, so that Christ may dwell in your hearts through faith. And I pray that you, being rooted and established in love, may have power, together with all the saints, to grasp how wide and long and high and deep is the love of Christ, and to know this love that surpasses knowledge—*that you may be filled to the measure of all the fullness of God* [emphasis mine]" (3:16–19).

Let that be your prayer. To be filled with the measure of all the fullness of God means no room for panic, no room for doubting Christ's bottomless love for you. His Spirit dwells in you, as he promises it will when you believe in Christ, giving you the power to live in certainty and joy.

Paul wrote in Hebrews that nothing in all creation is hidden from God's sight (4:13). Seeing you gripped by panic grieves God's heart. If Paul were here today, he would be excited to remind you of the words of Psalm 118: "The LORD is with me; I will not be afraid. What can man do to me? The LORD is with me; he is my helper. I will look in triumph on my enemies" (vv. 6–7).

Really what you're on is a search for wisdom that will empower you to live a life not ruled by panic. "For the LORD gives wisdom," writes Solomon in Proverbs 2:6–7a "and from his mouth come knowledge and understanding. He holds victory in store for the upright ..." Applying God's Word to your mind and heart is God's prescription for physical well-being: "This will bring health to your body and nourishment to your bones" (3:8).

Don't let panic distort the truth about you. God says you are his child and that he longs to help you live an abundant life. Trust him to be true to his Word.

Power Tools for Empowered Living

Often our ability to give and receive love and comfort is hampered by beliefs we hold. We think these beliefs make us stronger and better people. In reality, they weaken us. Because they are based on falsehood rather than truth and steal the power God gives us as his children, I like to call them "Power Padlocks."

For every Power Padlock there is a Power Principle or scriptural truth to counteract the lie. These scriptural truths are supported by the Bible verse listed in the Power Passage. Together they help you identify ways in your own life to apply the truths you have just discovered. Check out the Power Tools for panic below.

Power Tools

Power Padlock: If you knew the things I've done, you couldn't possibly love me.

Power Principle: There's no sin too big for God to forgive.

Power Passage: "And the prayer offered in faith will make the sick person well; the Lord will raise him up. If he has sinned, he will be forgiven. Therefore confess your sins to each other and pray for each other so that you may be healed. The prayer of a righteous man is powerful and effective. Confess your sins to each other that you may be healed (James 5:13–16).

Power Question: Why do I have difficulty acknowledging my weaknesses and confessing my sin to others?

Power Padlock: I haven't been loved in the past, so why would anyone love me now?

Power Principle: God has always loved you and created you to be loved.

Power Passage: "I have loved you with an everlasting love; I have drawn you with loving-kindness" (Jeremiah 31:3).

Power Question: How would my life be changed if I really believed God loves me?

Power Padlock: If you knew who I really am, you couldn't possibly love me.

Power Principle: God knows us completely and wants us to be known by others.

Power Passage: "O LORD, you have searched me and you know me. You know when I sit and when I rise; you perceive my thoughts from afar. You discern my going out and my lying down; you are familiar with all my ways. Before a word is on my tongue you know it completely, O LORD. You hem me in—behind and before; you have laid your hand upon me. Such knowledge is too wonderful for me ..." (Psalm 139:1–6).

Power Question: What is there about me that I feel I have to hide or camouflage from others?

Power Padlock: I believe I'm not worth loving, so why waste your time on me?

Power Principle: God made me worthy simply by creating me.

Power Passage: "I am fearfully and wonderfully made; your works are wonderful" (Psalm 139:14).

Power Question: What is there about me that makes me question God's design?

Obsessive Compulsive Disorder Self-Discovery Tool

Directions: Please answer "yes" or "no" to each of these questions. (The results of this self-discovery are for information purposes only. Please see a mental-health professional for diagnosis and treatment.)

1. Do you check and recheck the stove, locks, lights switches, iron, or the car emergency brake? Yes___ No___

2. Do you avoid dirt or germs? Yes___ No___

3. Do you fear the possibility of contamination? Yes___ No___

4. Have you expressed excessive concern about contracting or spreading an illness? Yes___ No___

5. Are you aware of right or left movement when you walk or talk? Yes___ No___

6. Have you experienced intrusive thoughts that you consider sexually shameful, violent, or bad? Yes___ No___

7. Are you ashamed of your thoughts about God or other religious figures? Yes___ No___

8. Do you obsess about your sin/badness? Do you think it is too much for God to forgive? Yes___ No___

9. Do you fear harming a loved one because you're not careful enough? Yes___ No___

10. Are you consumed with washing, personal grooming, or household cleaning? Yes___ No___

11. Do you do mental gymnastics with numbers, letters, or words, rearranging or reorganizing them into various patterns or categories? Yes___ No___

12. Do you track "lucky" numbers or act on superstitions? Yes___ No___

13. Do you struggle with giving away clothing, newspapers, or other items? Yes___ No___

14. Have you hoarded food, supplies, or other resources, fearing there will never be enough for you? Yes___ No___

15. Do you inspect the trash for valuable objects before taking it out? Yes___ No___

16. Are you overly attached to your possessions and do they function as a replacement for your extended family or significant relationships? Yes___ No___

17. Do you invest more than one hour a day performing any of these activities or rituals? Yes___ No___

18. Do you anticipate a sense of relief or a reduction of anxiety when performing these activities or rituals? Yes___ No___

If you answered yes to any of these questions, there is hope and help for you. Read on to learn more about OCD.

7 Obsessive Compulsive Disorder:
When You're Plagued by Not Being Perfect

"We have to go back to the house. I forgot to lock the door and turn off the stove," Jan demands of her husband, Matt, as they get into the car to go to the Christian counselor's office.

"No chance!" Matt replies. "You've checked everything three times already." He is exasperated by Jan. He loves her, but his patience is wearing thin.

How much more will I have to endure before Jan acknowledges her problem? Matt wonders. *I feel like I'm caught in an emotional tug-of-war. It seems like there are two different Jans,* Matt reflects. *There is the "real" Jan I've loved for many years and the ill one whose behavior is bizarre. I'm tired of watching her check and recheck the lights, and all her other checking/rechecking rituals. I hate seeing her binge and then hearing her purge. Sometimes the disgusting sound seems to rip open my own guts.*

For the past several years, Jan's anxieties have increased. They began in her childhood when problems surfaced in her father's ministry. Then he died suddenly before she could reconcile with him. She can't accept that he is dead and that she lost her opportunity to make peace with him. Her guilt continues to grow.

As the eldest sibling, Jan was the executor of the estate. She sold her father's home, but she didn't dispose of her father's personal property. All of his belongings were now stacked from floor to ceiling in Matt and Jan's house.

Anytime Matt so much as suggests that they get rid of the clutter, Jan refuses. The thought of removing these things triggers past feelings of abandonment that Jan can't bear to face.

Rather than reducing the clutter, she adds to it by frequently going to garage sales and bringing home other people's "stuff." Accumulating and hoarding possessions does nothing to alleviate her anxiety, but she does it anyway. Boxes of old bulletins from her father's church are piled on the kitchen counter, making it difficult for Jan and Matt to prepare meals. Stacks of Bible commentaries litter the dining room table making it impossible for them to eat dinner there. The house is almost bursting with secondhand junk, making upkeep and repairs nearly impossible.

In fact, the house is getting so run down, the neighbors have begun to drop comments to Matt, even calling into question Jan's mental stability. No one seems to understand that this disarray is her attempt to deal with her internal chaos and fear. Jan feels her mask of "normalcy" beginning to crack.

As Matt and Jan's car approaches the counseling office, Jan quietly counts backward from one hundred to reduce her growing anxiety: *One hundred, ninety-nine, ninety-eight, ninety-seven* ... Matt glances at Jan and notices her silently mouthing the words. He sees that her face has turned white with fear. *Another broken promise*, Matt assumes. *She said she didn't need to do that counting thing anymore.*

Jan looks apologetically at Matt and blurts out, "I can't go to the appointment."

Matt feels his anger swell as he pulls into the parking garage. He clenches his teeth and looks straight into her eyes. He has learned in counseling that he needs to be loving but firm. "I love you, but I will not live like this. I'm setting a boundary because I care about you. Unless you go to that appointment, we're going to have to separate."

Jan feels her stomach knot and her pulse race as she and Matt enter the office building. She desperately wants to escape the confrontation, but before Matt can say more, she grabs her stomach and tells him, "I'm getting sick; I need to go the restroom."

Matt carefully studies his wife as Jan hurries away down the hall. He marvels how her every movement is synchronized to accent her perfect figure. Her full head of auburn hair is held exactly in place. Her long, sculptured fingernails accent her lean body structure. No one would ever guess someone so beautiful could be in such emotional turmoil.

Jan enters the women's lounge and is relieved to find it empty. Her greatest fear is that someone will discover that her life is hopelessly out of control. She goes into the stall—sticks her fingers in her throat—presses her tongue down—and leans forward. *If only I weren't so fat, my husband would stay with me. I vowed I would never become obese like my mother. My father's affair would never have started if Mother had taken care of herself. I'm still angry with her. All the problems with his church and our friends were her fault!*

When Jan has completed her daily ritual with food, she goes to the sink to wash her hands. She turns on the water, waiting for it to become scalding hot, lathers her chapped hands, rinses them, and then repeats the ritualistic pattern ten more times.

Jan looks at her cracked and bleeding hands. A glance in the mirror shows her for the first time what her friends have been telling her for months. Her teeth are stained from the stomach acid that washes over them every time she "purges." Her once rosy cheeks are now hollow and sunken. *If I go in there like this,* Jan worries, *the therapist will surely know I have a problem. Still, I have to do this if I want to save my marriage.*

By the time Jan gets to the waiting room, Matt is already in the therapist's office. The counselor commences the session by asking specific questions to assess the magnitude of Jan's behavior. The various pieces of the familiar patterns of Obsessive Compulsive Disorder quickly emerge highlighting her guilt and shame.

What Is Obsessive Compulsive Disorder (OCD)?

According to the *Diagnostic and Statistical Manual for Mental Disorders (DSM-IV)* the important part of Obsessive Compulsive Disorder (OCD) is the "recurrent obsessions [and/] or common compulsions that are severe enough to be time consuming (i.e., they take more than one hour a day) or cause marked distress or significant impairment."[1]

At some point, the person with these obsessions or compulsions realizes these behaviors are abnormal. Washing your hands more than twenty times per day in bleach, fear of contracting an STD if you use the public restroom, or throwing away clothing after eating at a restaurant for fear of contamination—these are just a few examples of behaviors associated with OCD.

In the church, there is confusion about Obsessive Compulsive Disorder. OCD produces an inaccurate perception of God and salvation, and causes a person to experience a faith crisis. Often, well-meaning Christians confront this as a spiritual issue, adding to the person's already crippling load of false guilt and shame. Healthy caregivers need to understand OCD to properly care for those wounded by this disorder.

Take heart. We're going to examine this disorder together and see what can be done about it.

What Is the Difference between an Addiction and Obsessive Compulsive Disorder?

OCD has been around for hundreds of years, as long as human behavior has been studied. In the past, OCD was misunderstood and associated only with addictions such as compulsive sexual behavior, eating, gambling, and a host of other behaviors.

To many, the goal of the addict and the compulsive person appears to be the same. There is a difference, however. The addict receives pleasure when engaging in his addiction, but the person with Obsessive Compulsive Disorder receives a fraction of relief for his anxiety and emotional pain. Although there is a lessening for the moment, it does not fill the need. Both OCD and the addict receive only temporary pleasure. The person with OCD only further increases his distress, as these patterns may relieve anxiety in the short-term but only make them feel worse in the long-term. He only continues the cycle when he receives false hope and pain again. His anxiety increases—he feels guilt and shame—and he obsesses about not being worthy of God's love.

In moderate to severe cases, medication is necessary to deal with the genetic/biological part of this disorder. Medication helps the individual by 60–70 percent in a four to six month time span.[2] The remaining issues (in moderate to severe cases) need to be managed through therapy.

What Are Obsessions?

The DSM-IV explains, "Obsessions are persistent ideas, thoughts, impulses or images that are experienced as intrusive and inappropriate and that cause marked anxiety or distress."[3]

The term "obsession" comes from the Greek word meaning "besieged."[4] When obsessive thoughts come into your mind, you can't get them out. They besiege you until you feel as if you're going crazy. A woman, for example, might not be able to get a passionate love scene from a movie out of her mind. Her thought life is "besieged" by the image. Every time her husband touches her, she compares him to the idealized lover in the movie.

It is important to understand that obsessions are not composed of ordinary worries about life, such as marriage issues, parent-child problems, or career difficulties. They range from the mundane to significant thoughts or mental images of an "upsetting nature like violence, vulgarities, harm to self or harm to others. Obsessions may be special numbers, colors, or single words or phrases … sometimes even melodies."[5]

Some common examples of obsessions are:

- **Germs.** This person fears contamination and will avoid public restrooms, restaurants, and hotels. He fears food poisoning and may be an extremely picky eater, avoiding even whole categories of foods. He may only eat prepackaged foods from the original container, and use prepackaged disposable utensils.

- **Dirt.** This person washes her toilets three times a day, washes walls every day, dusts daily, and vacuums before and after every meal. She changes her clothing four times a day and launders each item separately.

- **Doubt.** This person doubts himself so much that he can't hold down a job, doesn't believe his wife could possibly love him, and his sense of unworthiness alienates his children. He doubts God and his salvation and usually has a faith crisis.

- **Order.** This person spends hours organizing and reorganizing canned food alphabetically. Her closet is arranged by color, type of clothing, and hangers must be an exact distance apart.

- **Symmetry.** This person hangs all pictures a specific distance from the ceiling, measures the distance between her flowers and the sidewalk, and rearranges her friends' knick-knacks to reflect perfect balance.

- **Repugnant sexual thoughts.** This person creates vivid, perverse sexual images in his mind and is repulsed if these thoughts are revealed to anyone, even to a therapist.

- **Repugnant religious thoughts.** This person thinks God does not love her and questions her salvation because of her evil thoughts. "I hate God" or "I'm blaspheming God" are common worries.

- **Prayer.** This person must use the "right" words, the "right" phrases, and pray for the "right" length of time.

- **Repugnant images.** This person thinks about repulsive or distasteful events, such as body parts found following an explosion.

- **Horrific images.** This person sees mental snapshots of car accidents, bombings, or natural disasters.

- **Violent images.** This person thinks excessively about death and dying.

- **Checking rituals.** This person fears forgetting to turn off the lights, lock the doors, or pick up children from school. He checks and rechecks to make sure everything's all right.

- **Fear that a mistake will harm a loved one.** This person fears that she may drop her newborn infant, cause a car accident by walking down the street, and kill her husband by undercooking meat. (This is not homicidal ideation because this person is terrified of hurting someone rather than looking forward to it. There is no rage involved.)[6]

The person with these obsessions knows they are irrational. They try to reduce obsessions by avoiding them or neutralizing them by using a compulsive behavior. Anxiety, for example, might be reduced by counting numbers back and forth in one's head or by counting the cracks in the sidewalks.

What Are Compulsions?

The DSM-IV states, "Compulsions are repetitive behaviors (e.g., hand washing, ordering, checking [doing and undoing]) or mental acts (e.g., praying, counting, repeating words silently [mental gymnastics]) the goal of which is to prevent or reduce anxiety or distress, not to provide pleasure or gratification. In most cases, the person feels driven to perform the compulsion to reduce the distress that accompanies an obsession or to prevent some dreaded event or situation.

"By definition, compulsions are either clearly excessive or are not connected in a realistic way with what they are designed to neutralize or prevent."[7] Obsessive Compulsive Disorder is not generally caused by a trauma, as in other anxiety disorders. It is rather an unhealthy way to cope with one's fears that build and disorganize with repetition.

Any behavior can be taken to an extreme to address a fear, but some of the most common ones include

- Washing Hands (Excessive)
- Showering
- Checking Locks
- Checking Stoves
- Touching Things
- Counting Items
- Ordering Things
- Cleaning Things
- Performing Silly Rituals

Healthcare providers agree that engaging in any of these activities for more than an hour per day is a red flag warranting further investigation into possible OCD.

People who engage in compulsive behaviors want to stop but can't. They see no other way to reduce their anxiety and so continue in this vicious cycle of trying to alleviate their pain with useless activity. In severe cases, medication is necessary to break the cycle. These repetitive behaviors become compulsions when they are done to an extreme. Hand washing is a good example. Many people with OCD, like Jan, wash their hands numerous times throughout the day in an attempt to reduce stress and anxiety.

How Common Is Obsessive Compulsive Disorder?

For years, OCD was considered a rare disease because people with symptoms hid their behaviors. A survey conducted by the National Mental Health Institute showed that OCD affects more than 2 percent of the population.[8] It is now considered more common than such severe mental illnesses as schizophrenia, bipolar disorder, or panic disorder. It equally affects men and women.

"Studies indicated that at least one-third of cases of Obsessive Compulsive Disorder in adults began in childhood. Suffering from OCD during early stages of a child's development can cause severe problems for the child,"[9] including difficulty completing an education and finding work in the teen and young adult years. Many of these children and adults are eventually classified as disabled.

Why Does Obsessive Compulsive Disorder Begin?

There are many theories about the origins of Obsessive Compulsive Disorder. Some researchers think the disorder is genetic. Others think OCD first develops in childhood as a result of anxiety that produces discomfort, which is reduced by a conditioned avoidance response. These avoidance responses take on the form of ritualistic behaviors that lay a foundation for OCD in adulthood.[10]

For example, a child who is nervous about going to school may count the cracks in the sidewalk as a means of reducing her fears. The behavior distracts her enough for her to believe that it has removed the fear. Thus, as she grows up, she associates counting things with relieving stress.

In moderate to severe cases where genetics are involved, medication is necessary to stabilize the condition.

Why Is Obsessive Compulsive Disorder Considered a Family Disease?

There is evidence that OCD, like other anxiety disorders, "runs in families."[11] Researchers aren't certain yet if the disorder is genetic, but 15 to 20 percent of OCD sufferers have an immediate family member with the disorder.

Obsessive Compulsive Disorder generally impacts the entire family. Family members are drawn into the OCD behavior and often become angry about the elaborate obsessions and compulsions that accompany this disorder.

For example, the morning commute is delayed when the family is held up by the son who insists on washing his hands several times before going to school. The family can't understand that he can't just stop the behavior and "get over it!"

What Is the Difference between Obsessive Compulsive Disorder and Obsessive Compulsive Personality Disorder?

People tend to confuse OCD with Obsessive Compulsive Personality Disorder (OCPD). OCPD is more concerned with order, control, and neatness. The woman looks forward to going home at night to clean her house or get things in order and receives pleasure from the task. She bases her self-esteem on the praise she receives from others for managing her well kept home. There is a general sense of security in being able to have control over all aspects of life. In contrast, the person with OCD does not find any pleasure or satisfaction from completing the tasks. It is a means of reducing her anxiety.

Why Does Obsessive Compulsive Disorder Need Relationship to Heal?

When we think of OCD, many of us remember the movie, *As Good as It Gets*. In this popular Hollywood film, Jack Nicholson plays a middle-aged bachelor diagnosed with OCD. He is consumed by an irrational fear of germs and wears leather gloves to protect his hands when in public.

Nicholson's rituals and compulsions are strange or bizarre. He is a lonely man because those outside his immediate community think his behavior is abnormal. The film illustrates that Obsessive Compulsive Disorder impairs one's life, career, and social relationships.

Nicholson sees a therapist and begins to get well. He meets Helen Hunt. One of my favorite scenes is when he enters a posh country club to impress her with his sophistication. The maître d' embarrasses Nicholson in front of Hunt by requiring him to wear a suit jacket to enter the establishment. The man with the black tie and tails hands him a blazer and instructs him to wear it over his shirt, but Nicholson refuses. He fears the others who had worn it before might have had germs.

Nicholson's unwillingness to wear the attire makes a scene in the restaurant. In the midst of all the chaos he notices that the other men's eyes are sizing up Hunt. He looks deeply into her sparkling eyes—he dashes out of the restaurant—and he races out to a store to purchase a new dinner jacket. When he returns later wearing a handsome sports jacket and matching tie, Hunt is impressed. She realizes he is going to great lengths to please her.

Why Do People with Obsessive Compulsive Disorder Need Relationship?

People with OCD need relationship to heal. But they are hurt and ashamed of their strange behavior. They think that if their rituals are exposed, people will label them "bad." To protect their tattered self-esteem, they often go to extremes by under- or overvaluing themselves.

The person who undervalues himself will withdraw from others and build an emotional wall or shell that no one can penetrate. He will isolate from others so that no one will see his behavior. I once heard of a man who wore mirrored sunglasses in the rain to cover his problem of blinking too much. He believed if others saw his problem, they would surely not want him as a friend. Healing came when he was able to take off his glasses and let others see his pain.

The person who overvalues herself will go to the other extreme by elevating or broadcasting her good for all to see. Counselors call this "egocentricity" or "grandiosity." These individuals are feeling worthless and frightened on the inside, but they present themselves as competent on the outside. This internal conflict creates stress and anxiety and causes those with Obsessive Compulsive Disorder to hide the flawed part of themselves, which further increases their anxiety.

If you attempt to show these people love, they will find a way to sabotage or destroy it. They generally undervalue themselves and believe they are unworthy, and unlovable, and unacceptable.

They need the reassurance of Jesus' words. "Accept one another, then, just as Christ accepted you, in order to bring praise to God" (Romans 15:7). Acceptance implies equality—all of us members of the same body of believers, each part of the body as important as any other.

Before I became a therapist I was a youth worker. One day a young woman asked if she could talk to me in private following a Bible study. Tears cascaded down her face as she told me that she liked one of the boys in our group.

The problem with the relationship was that he came from a well-established, affluent Christian family that she felt was superior to her humble roots. She felt she didn't measure up because she had been raped and was no longer a virgin. She was sure he would leave her when he found out the truth—she was "flawed" and no longer "perfect." She purposely started a disagreement over something trivial to push him away before he could reject her. She didn't think she was worthy of his love.

People with OCD feel inferior, ashamed, and frightened. In extreme cases they anticipate rejection and give up. They may develop suicidal thinking or engage in harmful behavior to destroy the bad part of them. They are afraid others will see their obsessions and compulsions and no longer love them. They're frantically searching for someone who will come alongside and say, "I love you *period*—in your good, bad, and ugly moments."

Why Do People with Obsessive Compulsive Disorder Need Love?

A girlfriend once gave me an orchid plant as a gift. She told me to water it regularly and to take good care of it. I thanked her for it and promised her, "I'll water it with my other houseplants every week."

"No! Orchids need more water than other plants to live."

"What do you mean?"

"They're planted in bark that absorbs the water," my friend explained. "If you pour a little water over the top of them like you do with your other plants, the water will just run through, and the bark will not soak it up."

"Put the stopper in your sink and fill it full of water," she instructed me. "Place the plant in the water and let it drink. Orchids are funny plants in that they need to be saturated with water."

My plant didn't live very long. I learned that orchids are hard to grow at home. But as a therapist, I learned a more important lesson about love. People who have anxiety disorders need to be saturated by the love of others in the body of Christ. One small drop of water once a week in church will not provide the love and emotional support they need for them to get well. They need a consistent flow of love to help them enhance their good parts and embrace their bad parts as they heal.

People with OCD need to take responsibility for their lives by setting personal boundaries. They need to develop a structure that enables them to seek comfort, acceptance, and love. People with OCD find it difficult to be part of a local church and to reach out socially. It is hard for them to allow others to see and know their bad parts. They need loving structure, support, and accountability to help them separate their personhood from their obsessions and compulsions, to break the cycle of Obsessive Compulsive Disorder, and begin trusting people again. They need to be in relationship with healthy Christians who can demonstrate appropriate boundaries.

The body of Christ has tremendous power to administer healing to those affected by Obsessive Compulsive Disorder.

David prayed for "an undivided heart" with which to praise the Lord and glorify his name, and from which to be distracted by no other thing. "For great is your love toward me; you have delivered me from the depths of the grave" (Psalm 86:13).

When attacked by enemies from within and without, David prayed this prayer: "But you, O Lord, are a compassionate and gracious God, slow to anger, abounding in love and faithfulness. Turn to me and have mercy on me; *grant your strength to your servant* [emphasis mine] and save the son of your maidservant" (vv. 15–16).

If you wish to be truly healthy in mind, body, and soul, you must draw close to God. He is Jehovah Jireh, the Great Provider. In his wisdom, he will meet your needs. Paul prayed that the Colossians would be :strengthened with all power according to his glorious might so that you may have great endurance and patience ..." (Colossians 1:11).

Be of good courage. God sees your struggle and wants to see you learn to manage it, not be controlled by it.

Power Tools

Power Padlock: I don't think anyone cares enough about me to love and accept me as I am.

Power Principle: God knew you and loved you before you were even born.

Power Passage: "I pray that you, being rooted and established in love, may have power to grasp how wide and long and high and deep is the love of Christ, and to know this love that surpasses knowledge" (Ephesians 2:18–19).

Power Question: Why can't I love myself? Why do I avoid people who love me?

Power Padlock: My compulsive behavior is too powerful for me to manage.

Power Principle: Using the principles discussed in this book, you can learn to manage your compulsions and live the life God has for you.

Power Passage: "His divine power has given us everything we need for life and godliness through our knowledge of him who called us by his own glory and goodness" (2 Peter 1:3).

Power Question: Why do I turn to a compulsive behavior to meet the needs that God has intended for either himself or another person to meet?

Power Padlock: If a person rejects me, my beliefs about my lack of value and worth will be confirmed.

Power Principle: You are a valuable person simply because of who you are: an individual created in the image of God.

Power Passage: "God created man in his own image, in the image of God he created him; male and female he created them" (Genesis 1:27).

Power Question: Why don't I want to believe God loves and values me?

Power Padlock: No one else had ever had to deal with the troubles and difficulties I'm facing right now.

Power Principle: Your experience may be more common than you would guess. How will you know for sure unless you seek out relationships with others?

Power Passage: "What has been will be again, what has been done will be done again; there is nothing new under the sun" (Ecclesiastes 1:9).

Power Question: Why am I unwilling to let others share in my struggles and difficulties?

Part 2 Strategies for Managing Anxiety Successfully

"We fear things in proportion to our ignorance of them.
Truth is often eclipsed but never extinguished."
—Unknown

R.E.L.A.X. to Reduce
Panic and Anxiety

R espond to anxiety by taking control of yourself and your fears; stop letting anxiety control you.

E ncourage your body to relax by way of diaphragmatic or deep breathing. Inhale; hold your breath while counting to twenty; exhale. Repeat three times. Practice deep breathing ten minutes a day for a minimum of six weeks.

L earn to relax through stretching, exercising large-motor muscle groups. (Pinpoint where your body carries stress and learn to consciously relax those muscles.) Take a hot bath or shower, develop a hobby, or listen to music. Meditate, pray, discipline your mind by using distraction or thought-stopping techniques. Don't forget, when you experience anxiety, your body is telling you it is overstressed. Ease tensions by getting regular sleep and eating a balanced diet.

A pply the principles of "systematic desensitization." Exposing yourself slowly to what you fear will bring healing. If you fear going to a new church, for example, begin by going into the church and staying for the music. Increase your time at church slowly, by staying for a few extra minutes each week until you feel comfortable to stay for the entire service.

X -ray your fears. Be willing to examine the possible sources of rejection, including a controlling parent or critical adult figure. Take a risk to let others love your imperfect parts; stop isolating.

8 Deep Breathing and Other Relaxation Techniques:
Reducing the Effects of Anxiety

Steve, Jan, Sarah, Paula, Christina, and Mike have all gone through the initial intake process with Debbie, a licensed mental health counselor. Each has received his or her diagnosis and had the opportunity to receive initial information about their disorder and ask questions.

They've each had an opportunity to understand their specific anxiety diagnoses during several individual sessions with the therapist. The characters now come together in a group setting that continues for a year to learn more about the specific skills that apply to each of their anxiety disorders.

For some people, group therapy is the quickest intervention for anxiety disorders because of the intensity and focus on relational issues. In group, individuals work on relational issues with their therapist and with other group members. For example, we might have a man who hates women find himself in a group full of women. In group he will have to work on interacting with female members in an appropriate way.

We will follow Debbie as she encourages members to establish boundaries, manage their anxiety, and reach out to others for their relational needs.

"Anxiety is a monster that grows every time you feed it with avoidance," Debbie explains to the members during the first session of the anxiety group.

"The more you let yourself get anxious without managing it," Debbie continues, "the more severe the anxiety becomes. Every time you let it go and avoid it, it will get worse." All group members are listening intently to the teaching on relaxation techniques and are actively taking notes as Debbie teaches the group about anxiety.

> "Panic and anxiety no longer have to control you, but you can control them."

"Panic and anxiety are not suddenly eliminated," Debbie points out, "but they reduce gradually over time. You can learn how to manage them." She shifts her focus away from the group to note the time on the wall. She is conscious of keeping a good time boundary as an example to the group.

"For instance, if you're diabetic, you must learn to manage your glucose or blood sugar levels. If you have high blood pressure, you learn to monitor it and reduce your salt intake. If you have anxiety, you must learn to manage it and control your body." Debbie pauses before she continues. "Panic and anxiety no longer have to control you, but you can control them." Debbie notes that Paula's eyes have widened, her skin is turning white, and she appears to be gasping for breath.

Paula frantically interrupts Debbie. "I need to get out of here—I feel as if I can't breathe—I'm losing control and everything is closing in on me.

Debbie puts down her notes and focuses on Paula.

"I know something is wrong with me," Paula exclaims. "I feel as if I can't breathe—I feel my heart beating fast—I think I'm having a heart attack." Paula quickly gets up from her chair, darts toward the door. "I'm going to the ER; I'm sure there's something wrong with my heart."

Debbie asks Paula to stop for a moment. "There is one question I want to ask you first. Do you feel as if you're choking or gagging?"

A look of surprise appears on Paula's face. She stops and asks, "How did you know what I'm feeling?"

"Because that's panic," Debbie informs Paula. "The ER doctor diagnosed you with it and I concur with his evaluation. You're having a panic attack."

Paula looks at Debbie in disbelief. "Is this what one feels like? I've had these for years."

Debbie nods and reassures Paula, "Yes, this is what panic feels like."

Paula breaths a deep sigh of relief. Suddenly memories of the ER doctor flood her mind. She remembers a nicely dressed middle-aged man telling her she didn't have a heart problem, but she did have Panic.

"I know the ER doctor told me I have Panic," Paula recalls, "but why do I feel like I'm going to die?"

"That's one of the symptoms of panic," Debbie answers. "People usually know something is wrong, but they don't know what to do with these symptoms. Many go to the ER thinking they are having heart problems, but their symptoms generally subside in five to thirty minutes when it's Panic.

"Let me assure you," Debbie continues, "you're not going to die. But, you do have a problem with panic. This is an ideal opportunity to learn how to manage your panic in the context of the group."

"I want to get over this," Paula explains as she takes her seat. She looks desperately into Debbie's eyes and pleads, "Will you help me? I want to get over this—I'm tired of feeling out of control. I'm always afraid because I never know when I'll have my next attack."

"There is hope," Debbie reassures her again. "You can learn to manage your anxieties and live a normal life."

"Are you serious? I'm skeptical," Paula confides to Debbie. "I've never known anyone who's as anxious as I am."

Tools for Relaxation

1. Diaphragmatic or deep breathing
2. Muscle relaxation
3. Mind discipline
4. Prayer and meditation
5. Hot bath or shower
6. Walking, swimming or another form of exercise
7. Hobbies or fun activities
8. Rocking in a chair, listening to music, or reading a book
9. Eating healthy, well-balanced meals
10. Adequate sleep

"Yes, Paula. Many others have experienced panic and have been able to find help through these proven techniques."

Debbie's confident answer brings color back to Paula's pale face. She is ready to listen to the counselor.

Before Debbie can continue, Christina voices her confusion about anxiety and her own diagnosis. "Do I have Panic? I don't think I've ever been diagnosed with it, but I have some of Paula's symptoms."

"Your symptoms are less severe," Debbie explains to Christina. "You have Generalized Anxiety Disorder. As we work with your disorder in our group, you'll notice that you share many of the symptoms of the other disorders. Your symptoms weren't acute and specific enough to warrant another diagnosis."

Debbie pauses for a moment before addressing the whole group, "To get well, you'll need to learn to manage your anxiety with deep breathing and other relaxation techniques. In other sessions, we'll make specific applications to your individual anxiety disorders. There are some specific differences in how these tools are applied to Obsessive Compulsive Disorder, Posttraumatic Stress Disorder, and the other disorders.

"Deep breathing is one of the most important methods that you all can use to reduce your anxiety," Debbie continues.

"What do you mean, 'deep breathing'?" Christina asks. "This sounds like childbirth class to me." Debbie reminds Christina that they have discussed this technique during their individual counseling sessions.

"Let's start practicing now by tuning in to your body. Everybody, sit up in your chair. Now exhale. Inhale deeply from your diaphragm and hold it to my count of 15 if you can. ... 6, 7, 8, 9, ... Steve, how are you doing? You look a little flushed. Exhale if you need to." Debbie has the group repeat the exercise three times.

"Do any of you notice a difference in your anxiety level?" About three quarters of the group raise their hands.

Debbie encourages the rest of the group to do deep breathing twice a day for ten minutes at a time for four to six weeks. "Some of you are so stressed, it will take that long for you to feel relief. The best time to do it is in the morning when you wake up and at night before you go to sleep. If you are not a morning or late-night person, you might want to do it at lunch or dinner."

Steve complains. "Six weeks! That feels like an eternity!"

But Debbie replies, "Some people aren't as fortunate as you are, Steve. Your doctor has told me he doesn't think you'll need medication if you practice deep breathing consistently as he prescribed. Wouldn't you rather do this than take medication? This way is more natural and much less expensive. Of course, I don't want to overlook the obvious. It is important to give your body what it needs to relax. A good diet, regular exercise, and sufficient sleep can make a significant difference."

Sarah sighs, shifting side to side in her chair.

"Thanks for that reminder, Sarah," Debbie quips. "Many of you may not be aware that sighing is another natural way the body releases tension. It's a little like a release valve on a pipe. When pressure builds to dangerous levels, the valve regulates the stress on the pipe. When you hear yourself sigh, it is a signal that your body is stressed and needs to relax. God has designed our bodies with a natural release valve—sighing—that allows us to naturally reduce our anxieties and stress."

Then Debbie goes on to discuss other natural methods God has designed to help us let go of our stress, tension, and anxiety.

What Is Diaphragmatic Breathing?

Football players have a saying they use often, "A good defense makes a good offense." In our game plan to win against anxiety, diaphragmatic or deep breathing is the first line of defense.

Deep breathing can be used by itself or in conjunction with medication. In fact, you may find that you'll use the techniques for the rest of your life to reduce your anxiety. For those with less severe cases and who prefer not to use medication, they first try deep breathing as a natural alternative.

Deep breathing doesn't cost anything, but it does take a little time and effort to practice. It should be utilized twice a day for ten minutes each time and as needed throughout the day to condition the body to relax. Sometimes a person may need to do these exercises for a period of a month or longer before relief begins. Consistency in practicing is critical to helping your body relax.

No matter how consistent you are, however, deep breathing will not be effective unless you breathe from your diaphragm. Most people over five years old tend to be self-conscious about letting their abdomens relax and "hang out" and have lost the ability to breathe in this healthy way. If your tummy is not going out on your inhale and in on your exhale, you are not breathing correctly. To practice this technique, lie on the floor and put a book on your abdomen directly under your ribcage. When you inhale, the book should rise, and when you exhale it will come down again.

Deep breathing needs to be incorporated into your lifestyle as a daily habit. It should also be used when you become nervous and overwhelmed during the course of the day. If you become anxious before speaking, deep breathing is a natural process that can be done on the way to the podium. If anxiety develops when you're driving, pull off to the side of the road and begin the process. If your husband is upset with you, you can ask for a time out and follow this simple process before returning to the conversation. Deep breathing is a simple way to manage anxiety and retrain your body to relax.

What Are Other Lines of Defense Against Anxiety?
Muscle Relaxation

There are multiple methods of muscle relaxation. Stretching and large-motor movements, such as arm or leg circles, are helpful and often bring immediate relief. People with anxiety disorders need structured, systematic relaxation that focuses on tensing and releasing different muscle groups.

Another tool to relax muscles is warm water. For many people taking a warm bath or shower or sitting in a hot tub is soothing. Since overcoming my fear of water as a youth, I love to swim laps. One of my favorite parts of this exercise is rewarding myself by sitting in a hot tub, talking and laughing with others. As the warm water washes over my body, it helps to relax tight muscles.

Mind Discipline

Disciplining the mind involves setting limits on your thoughts. Distracting techniques help your mind mentally disengage from your environment and see yourself in a more pleasant setting. Recently a friend of mine had an invasive medical procedure. Her doctor instructed her to imagine she was on a warm, sunny beach in Hawaii to distract herself from what was going on around her. This technique got her through a procedure she had feared and dreaded.

"Thought-stopping" techniques involve training the mind to turn off the "worry machine." For example, if you are worried about your finances, you would choose to stop thinking about money and refocus on your relationship with God and the spiritual blessings you've been freely given.

Writers in the Book of Psalms have recorded what many have known throughout the ages—that meditation and prayer are a means of achieving inner peace and relaxation. Neurologists have been able to measure the relaxing effect of meditation on both mind and body. This technique requires self-discipline and six to twelve months of practice to be effective.

What Are Other Relaxation Techniques?

There is a fourth line of defense used in managing anxiety. Try the following relaxation techniques to see which ones work best for you, since not every technique will work for everyone.

1. **Hobbies or fun activities.** Focusing on an activity that you consider fun can reduce anxiety. During my mother's twelve-year battle with breast cancer and another rare physical disease, she took up china painting, a hobby she had enjoyed several years before. Whenever she received bad news from her oncologist, she and I would sit and paint. I don't have an artistic bent, and I never progressed very far, so instead, I turned to writing and began to publish in Christian magazines. I found that writing was an enjoyable activity that helped others and relieved some of my stress during her illness. It also allowed me to get in touch with feelings that I couldn't express in any other way.

2. **Rock in a chair, read, and listen to music.** When I had some problems with my back several years ago and couldn't sleep at night, my physical therapist told me to get out of bed and rock in a chair. I would read, listen to music, and rock. It helped to relax me. All three of these activities engage the brain in a way different from worrying.

3. **Watch a sunset, drive in the mountains, or take a walk in the woods.** In the Pacific Northwest, we are blessed with pristine saltwater beaches, rugged mountains, and unspoiled forests. I enjoy the outdoors and look forward to walking with friends on the paths near my home. I love the

scent of fresh air following the rain. It calms my weary soul and refreshes my body.

4. **Healthy lifestyle.** I know that a good night's sleep makes all the difference in how I handle times of great stress. Good nutrition and regular exercise give me the energy I need to do what God has called me to do. For those with anxiety disorders, a healthy lifestyle includes avoiding alcohol, caffeine in all forms (chocolate, soda, coffee, and some teas), and illegal drugs. While these substances are often used as a form of self-medication and may appear to improve a person's condition, they tend to increase anxiety and the possibility of addiction over time.

Why Are Medications Sometimes Used with Anxiety Disorders?

Medications are considered another line of defense in the battle against anxiety. In the case of Obsessive Compulsive Disorder, for example, medication is most likely needed, along with relaxation tools, to help you manage your anxiety.

Medication is also used when other techniques are not working fast enough. Again, it is not unusual for relaxation techniques to take up to thirty days to take effect. Your medical doctor or a psychiatrist can discuss with you the advantages and disadvantages to using anti-anxiety medication. There are certain medications that work better with each individual disorder. We will be discussing this at length in chapter 10.

Why Is "Adult Responsibility" Needed to Overcome Panic and Anxiety?

For any of these anti-anxiety techniques to work, you must take adult responsibility for your life. If you want to recover, you have to be willing to do the work. You can't rely on others to do it for you.

Stewardship is defined as "the individual's responsibility to manage his life … with proper regard to the rights of others."[1] To be a good steward, we must learn to be responsible for every aspect of our lives—including an anxiety disorder.

You can choose to live in anxiety or you can stand up, fight back, and overcome your disorder. *You can gain power over panic and receive answers for anxiety.*

How Does Stewardship Relate to Anxiety?

When I was a little girl on the farm, my father had a friend named Pat. As a younger man Pat had raised livestock, but then he retired and moved to the city.

On a whim, Pat participated in a contest that required participants to guess the weight of a particular pig. Pat guessed 247 pounds, and the hefty animal weighed 247 pounds. Pat won the pig, but he had a problem. He lived in a small house in the city and didn't have a place for a pig. Pat asked my father for help.

"Your kids need an animal to teach them responsibility," Pat persuaded Father. "It would help Carol overcome her fear of animals. And besides, if they'll raise it, you can have half of the meat."

As a young child, I was stubborn and already set in my ways. When Father told me about it, I protested, "I don't want to raise it!"

Father was firm but loving in his response to me. I had recently experienced the death of my aunt and two uncles, and my parents figured I needed to spend more time with the animals to overcome my fear and give me something to care for during my grieving period. Father asked my brother and me to go with Pat to look at the pig.

When I finally saw her, my little heart pounded—the noise from her snout scared me. But something in her big brown eyes reached beyond my tough exterior, and the pig won her way into my heart. I studied her body and marveled at her beautiful hide glistening in the sun.

When I got close to her, a strange odor overpowered me. I took another breath and realized it was coming from the pig. I determined if I were going to have her she was going to be kept clean. I didn't know it at the time, but clean is not the natural state of pigs. Pat told me it was going to take some real hard work on my part to keep her clean. If she would belong to my brother and me, we'd have to be responsibile to care for her. My brother and I rose to the challenge and agreed to take the pig.

When we got home, the first thing we had to do was to build a pen for the pig. We placed it on the edge of the property, away from everything else. A man delivered her to us in a special truck. In honor of our friend Pat, my brother and I affectionately called her "Patricia."

Mother took my brother and me to the feed store where we got grain. But before long, we learned pigs also need fresh vegetables and fruits. We made arrangements with a local grocery store to get leftovers. Every couple of days, my brother and I had to go to the store for these items.

As time went on, Patricia started to eat more and more. I couldn't seem to get her enough food to eat. We asked our friend Pat to come and look at the pig. When he saw her, he started to laugh. He took my brother and me aside and politely explained to us that our pet pig was pregnant.

We began to prepare for the birth of Patricia's children. Every day after school, I rushed home to change my clothes and immediately went to her pen to see how her body was changing. I learned much about life from my pig.

Finally the big day came. Mother was waiting for my brother and me at the bus stop. She rushed us to Patricia, who was giving birth to the final piglet. She had twelve of the most adorable babies I'd ever seen. With soft pink hides and curly tails, my heart melted at the sight of them. Patricia looked directly at me. I reached over and put my hand on her hide and congratulated her. I somehow knew she was proud of her lot, and it was important to her that I thought well of her.

I carefully watched as she began the process of cleaning the babies with her tongue. Although pigs are known to be dirty animals, she was meticulous about the care of her children. When the novelty of the new pigs wore off, my brother and I realized we had a problem. Instead of finding food for one animal, now we had thirteen. I soon realized that caring for thirteen pigs was a lot more work than caring for one.

One night, a coyote hungry for a fresh pork dinner, stalked the piglets. Fortunately the barking of my dog, Susie, alerted my father who jumped out of bed and chased the coyote away. The next day, he took us with him as we prepared to build a larger pen. The pen was like a natural boundary. It was a tool that kept the bad coyote out, and it also kept the little ones in where they would be safe.

Caring for Patricia and her piglets was an early lesson in stewardship. As responsible stewards of the animals, my brother and I had to take adult responsibility to care for our pigs and to establish boundaries to protect the animals.

What Is the Relationship Between Anxiety and Adult Authority?

God has given each of us a life to manage. We need to address our problems by establishing healthy boundaries, keeping the bad out and the good in.

Those who struggle with anxiety need to learn to use deep breathing and other relaxation techniques to overcome their fears. Sometimes that will mean setting aside time to practice deep breathing on a daily basis. Other times it will mean establishing a boundary to have enough time away from work to go for a walk or go to sleep early.

To gain power over anxiety, people with anxiety disorders must learn to practice these tools on a regular basis.

Often people say these tools don't work. Rather, what I have found is that people are not putting forth the effort to practice these techniques to manage their anxiety on a daily basis.

If you or someone you care about has an anxiety disorder, it is important to remember that anxiety can be managed. I tell my patients, "You have a choice: You can remain a victim and blame God and others for your anxiety, or you can take responsibility for your life and change it. You can either learn to manage your anxiety, or allow it to manage you.

"If you choose to stay imprisoned by your disorder, your life and relationships will be governed by anxiety and despair. If you choose to escape your self-made prison and trust God to overcome your anxiety, your life will be broadened and enhanced by new experiences and loving relationships. You will be free to live life as God intended."

To see yourself through the lens of Jesus Christ, as God sees you, can make a tremendous difference in how well you manage your anxiety.

Perspective is critical.

Our museums are filled with items of historical significance excavated from the dump sites of ancient civilizations. The ancestors who threw out what they thought of as their trash did not have the perspective of time. They did not perceive how their castoffs could provide succeeding generations with so meaningful a window into their world.

For you to take authority and control over your anxiety, you need God's perspective on yourself. To the Colossians, Paul put it succinctly: "Once you were alienated from God and were enemies in your minds because of your evil behavior. But now he has reconciled you by Christ's physical body through death to present you holy in his sight, without blemish and free from accusation—if you continue in your faith, established and firm, not moved from the hope held out in the gospel" (Colossians 1:21–23a).

Be established and firm in faith. "Let the peace of Christ rule in your hearts, since as members of one body your were called to peace. And be thankful" (Colossians 3:15). By Christ's strength, his peace can rule in your heart because you *were called to peace!*

Power Tools

Power Padlock: It is too much work to manage my anxiety.

Power Principle: I need to be willing to put some effort into managing my anxiety.

Power Passage: "Do your best to present yourself to God as one approved, a workman who does not need to be ashamed and who correctly handles the word of truth" (2 Timothy 2:15).

Power Question: Where can I begin with the process of desensitization today?

Power Padlock: It is too complicated to learn to control my anxiety.

Power Principle: God will honor your hard effort in overcoming panic and anxiety.

Power Passage: "Lazy hands make a man poor, but diligent hands bring wealth" (Proverbs 10:4).

Power Question: Why am I resistant to trust God with this area of my life?

Power Padlock: I don't need a plan to manage my anxiety; I'll simply trust God.

Power Principle: God intends for us to be in relationship with him and with others.

Power Passage: "God had planned something better for us so that only together with us would they be made perfect" (Hebrews 11:40).

Power Question: How can I partner with God to fight my anxiety disorder?

Power Padlock: I can do the process of desensitization on my own. I don't need anyone.

Power Principle: It is helpful to have an accountability person to speak the truth to me and help me start the process of desensitization.

Power Passage: "Speaking the truth in love, we will in all things grow up into him who is the Head, that is, Christ" (Ephesians 4:15).

Power Question: Am I willing to listen when someone speaks the truth to me about my anxiety or panic?

The following is a list of fears that may be addressed through systematic desensitization.

Driving over bridges or through tunnels

Elevators, escalators, or stairs

Shopping in the mall or grocery store

Eating out in a restaurant or someone's home

Navigating and driving to new places or surroundings

Speaking or performing in public

Insects, snakes, and rodents

Traveling on an airplane, boat, or train

Invasive medical procedures

Zeroing in on animals

Attending a social function or group gathering alone

Touch or hugs

Illness or death

Openness about your opinions

Nervousness during tests or exams

9 Systematic Desensitization:
Learning to Manage Your Anxiety

"I'm scared I'm going to lose my job!" Jan tells the group. "I had to give a presentation yesterday, and I made a total fool of myself. Someone asked me a question I couldn't answer, and one of my overheads was missing.

"I really thought I was prepared. I'd done the research—and I thought my notes were organized, and I had practiced several times. I went home and ate everything in sight—a cake, a pepperoni pizza, a bag of potato chips, and four Dove bars—you name it, I ate it." The therapy group members glance nervously at each other, shocked by Jan's confession.

"The more I ate, the worse I felt about myself. I went into the bathroom— I looked at myself in the mirror—and I purged my food. I washed my hands again and again, but nothing seemed to help. I still feel so ashamed. I just can't accept my failures.

"Christina, can you accept me even though I just told you that I consumed the entire contents of my refrigerator in one sitting? Does it matter to you that I failed in my presentation at work?"

"Your failures—eating or speaking or whatever—don't affect my opinion of you," Christina replies. "I know what it's like to desire to be perfect. People have high expectations for doctors' wives. I feel like I'm always being measured against a scale of public opinion. I can never be thin enough, pretty enough, or spiritual enough."

"Can I comment here?" Steve asks. "I-I-I understand your pain over your speech at work—I have a communications disorder—I have a really hard time talking to p-p-p-people—I only wish I could get through a whole conversation

Steps to Desensitization

Acknowledge your anxieties to others.

Focus your energy on one source of anxiety.

Ask a counselor, spouse, or friend to help you.

Develop a plan.

Relax and visualize yourself doing what you fear.

Expose yourself to your anxiety in small increments.

Repeat the activity on your own.

Persevere in tackling your anxiety.

Treat yourself to a reward.

without stuttering."

Mike interrupts. "I don't like talking to people, either. I'd rather let my fist do the talking."

Debbie intervenes with Mike. She firmly holds to the structure of the group. "Mike, I appreciate your comments, but you need to wait for Jan to ask you a question since she has the floor. If you respond to her before she addresses you, you are 'care taking' for her by providing empathy and support she didn't ask for. Also ask yourself whose needs were you meeting with your comment: yours or hers? Were you helping Jan by your reply, or were you hoping the group would respect you more because you're a 'tough, macho guy'? Do you think you're above asking to have your needs met?"

Mike falls silent for a moment. "I don't understand what it means to ask for my needs to be met."

"Are you *asking* me to further explain to you about needs?" Debbie clarifies.

Mike is used to being in control, and his lack of understanding embarrasses him. "Yes, Debbie. Will you explain more about how to ask for what we need?"

"Mike, great job! You just asked me to meet a need."

"Is it that simple?"

"Yes, it is!" Debbie encourages. "But it's like learning to drive a car; it takes time and practice to feel comfortable doing it." Debbie goes on to explain to Mike the concept of asking for help to meet needs. She frames her comments in a way that will help Mike understand his inability to be direct about his needs.

Then Debbie redirects the conversation to Jan. "You've had some difficulty asking others for your needs in the past."

"But it feels so silly and unnatural to ask," Jan protests.

"It feels unnatural," Debbie elaborates further, "because we're afraid of taking the risk of getting hurt again. Many of us have been abandoned or betrayed—either physically or emotionally—by someone who we thought loved us. Even though it's hard to do, the bottom line is that you have to become vulnerable to others to have your needs met and experience love.

The group appears puzzled by this concept so Debbie elaborates. "Look at my hand," she says as she holds up her closed fist. "This represents your heart that has grown bitter, callous, and cold—closed to love." She reaches over, picks up a pen from the table, and tries to force it into her closed hand.

"I can't push this pen into my fist any more than a person can push love into a closed heart. But when I extend my fingers, one by one, starting with my pinkie, I can take in 'love'—in the form of this pen—little pieces at a time. When my hand is open, I can receive, hold on to, and value what I've been given. When our hearts open to love, we are able to utilize its power as we heal and grow.

"Jan, I'll not force you to do something you don't want to do, but I think it would be good for you to practice by asking the other group members the same question you asked Christina. It might help you to overcome your perfection-ism and understand that people value you beyond your performance."

Jan reluctantly agrees to ask the group members as Debbie has directed her.

"Mike, how do you feel about public speaking?" Jan asks.

"I avoid it as much as possible," Mike answers, "especially if I have to go somewhere I've never been. I'm afraid of going into unfamiliar surroundings because I never know when I might have a flashback. I can't control the sights, scents, or sounds that might trigger a bad memory."

"Paula, how do you feel about speaking in public?" Jan asks.

"I don't have to do it often, but I'm always afraid I'm going to be called on to pray in Bible study," Paula explains. "What if I have a panic attack? What would people think if they saw me come unglued?"

"Christina, what are your thoughts?" Jan asks.

"I dread being called on to read the Bible out loud in church," Christina responds. "I worry that I'll mispronounce one of those Old Testament names. Afterward, when I go to bed at night, I worry that I made a fool of myself; I replay the scene over and over in my mind."

"What about you, Jan?" Christina continues. "You're so beautiful and you seem so confident. It seems silly for someone like you to be so nervous about speaking in public."

Jan turns toward Debbie, hoping for affirmation. "Do you think my fear is silly?" she asks.

"Absolutely not, Jan," Debbie replies. "Your fear is real, and you're here because it's controlling your life. If you're willing to put some time and effort into it, I think a technique called 'systematic desensitization' can help. Would you like to hear more?"

"I'm already doing diaphragmatic breathing twice a day as well as the other relaxation techniques you recommended. This sounds like one more thing to do. Is it really worth my time?" questions Jan.

"It's definitely worth your time, and it *will* take some work on your part." Debbie states. "It will not only help you overcome your fear of giving a less-than-perfect presentation, it can also help address your Obsessive Compulsive Disorder."

Then Debbie turns to the other group members to include them in the discussion. "Paula, this technique could also be useful to address your Panic; Sarah, it could help you manage your phobias; and Christina, it could relieve your constant fear about the future. Steve and Mike, desensitization will help you as well. Along with deep breathing, thought-stopping, muscle relaxation, and meditation—which we've discussed in past group sessions—desensitization is another primary tool for the management of Anxiety."

"What do we have to do?" Jan asks Debbie. "You know I can't do anything unless I understand it first. I need exact details."

"Systematic desensitization is used to slowly expose a person to what he or she fears. The best way I can describe it is from a scene I saw on one of those emergency room programs. One night the program focused on a character who was a famous brain surgeon.

"This young brain surgeon, Greg, had a stroke at age forty. The effects of the stroke left him unable to perform surgery. Not wanting to lose a brilliant doctor, the hospital chief of staff offered Greg a position as a psychiatrist. This meant he would have to start over as an intern, but Greg was quite confident he could handle this new challenge.

"On his first day, the 'intern' was faced with a patient who was anxious in elevators. Greg was determined to show his supervisor how quickly he could get results, but he had to learn that people's emotional scars couldn't be healed in a few hours on an operating table like the physical ailments he had been treating.

"Greg's work at desensitization with this patient was agonizingly slow. His surgical training had not prepared him for relating to people on an emotional level. He and the patient labored session by session to overcome the phobia.

"At the first session, Greg laid out the treatment plan that would help the patient systematically face his anxiety in small increments. In the second session, Greg had his patient stand in front of the elevator and visualize riding in it. During the third session, Greg had him go inside the elevator and simply stand. For the fourth session, the patient actually got inside the elevator and closed the door, without going up or down. The next session, the patient rode to the second floor. Each subsequent week, he rode to the next floor higher. Therapy ended when he traveled to the ninth floor by himself. Both Greg and his patient felt as if they had climbed Mount Everest; they had accomplished their goal, and success was theirs."

"Wow! What a great story, but that was TV, and this is reality. Will this really work for us?" Jan asks hesitantly.

"Yes, I believe it will." Debbie says confidently.

What Is Systematic Desensitization?

"Desensitization is a process of unlearning the connection between anxiety and a particular situation."[1] Webster further explains desensitization as a process that makes an individual "insensitive or nonreactive to a sensitizing agent."[2] The process is also referred to as "exposure" or "exposure therapy" in psychological literature.

How Does Systematic Desensitization Work?

Pollen is an example of a sensitizing agent. My parents grew white Easter lilies each year in their greenhouse, and the yellow stamen (the part of the flower that holds the pollen) had to be removed before the plants could be sold. My mother had great difficulty working with the lilies because of her allergies to the pollen. Her nose ran, her eyes watered, and she sneezed uncontrollably whenever she was around these plants. To desensitize herself to the effects of the pollen, she took an allergy pill. The medication became the agent that allowed her body to become desensitized to the effects of the pollen through limited exposure for a longer period of time.

If you have an anxiety disorder, systematic desensitization can be your "allergy pill." The goal of this process is to get you to reduce your negative reactions to your anxieties. With time, positive experiences can overshadow negative ones when positive rewards are used as reinforcements. This process allows you to experience power over your anxieties and struggles.

When Can Systematic Desensitization Help?

One of my favorite desserts is blackberry pie with rich vanilla ice cream cascading over the crust. When I was a child, we would often go to the nearby blackberry patch to pick. The berries were very tiny, so picking them was no small feat, but well worth the effort when we ate this dessert.

On a bright August morning, I remember getting up early to go blackberry picking with my mother and a group of women from our community. One ambitious woman spent most of the morning filling a gallon bucket with the delicious berries. She seldom stopped to talk or stretch like the rest of us did.

When her bucket was nearly overflowing, she leaned down to pick the last few berries. Instead of berries, however, she grabbed a snake. She screeched and jumped back. The entire bucket of berries spilled into the bushes and tall grass. She cried from fright as well as frustration as she tried in vain to retrieve her morning's work.

As time went by, the woman told the story over and over. The attention and sympathy she got reinforced her behavior. Now, knowing that people will accommodate her fear, she refuses to go on camping trips or even to the zoo because she "might" see a snake. On one level, she wants to be rid of her phobia; on another level she is being rewarded for it. This woman's responses are common, and many health-care providers' experiences support the theory that an anxiety disorder could be learned behavior. If she were my patient, I would use systematic desensitization to help her break this behavioral cycle.

How Does Systematic Desensitization Help?

Desensitization is a tool that primarily helps those with an anxiety disorder expose themselves to what they fear.

If you are afraid of snakes, for example, desensitization can help you reduce your anxiety of serpents. Your therapist would likely start by encouraging you to go with a friend to the entrance of the reptile house at the zoo. Sit on the bench with your friend. Relax for ten or fifteen minutes. Ask your friend to talk to you about what it would be like to go inside. The next step would be for the two of you to go inside for a short period of time. Your third trip to the reptile house would involve picking a snake to look at for a short period of time. The following trip you would look at two snakes. The next time you would go through the entire reptile collection. The next stage is to repeat these steps by yourself. Once you reached this stage, the next step would be to go to a pet store where you would actually hold a snake.

If you're anxious when you drive over bridges or fly in a plane, desensitization will help you reduce that fear by exposing you to bridges or flying in much the same way as the person above was exposed to snakes.

The greatest challenge with this process is that it requires work on the patient's part. If you choose to use this form of therapy, you might have to endure some temporary discomfort and invest some time in exposing your fears.

Why Is Systematic Desensitization the Treatment of Choice?

Desensitization is the single most successful treatment for anxiety disorders because it's been proven to work! Research suggests that between fifty and sixty percent of an anxious person's symptoms can be reduced through desensitization. This form of treatment also has been proven to have the lowest relapse rate of any therapy, including medication.[3] (Although medication offers the quickest improvement rate, there is great potential for relapse if medication is not slowly reduced over time or when not taken as prescribed. See chapter 10 for more information on medication.)

How Did the Process Develop?

The study of desensitization and conditioning began many years ago with Russian physiologist Ivan Pavlov's well-known experiment with his dog. Pavlov rang a bell just before he fed the dog every day. In time the animal anticipated his food and began to salivate when he heard the bell. The results of this experiment eventually led other researchers to wonder if humans would react in a similar manner.

A few years later, Joseph Wolpe applied this process to helping people overcome their phobias. He found that desensitizing could be done mentally before a person physically approached the feared object or situation. He helped people relax while visually associating their anxieties with feelings of relaxation.

He believed that part of the battle included the anticipation of doing something that made a person anxious. Those who fear going to the dentist experience "anticipatory anxiety" of the drill and the needle long before they ever sit in the chair. Using Wolpe's method, a therapist would encourage someone to see himself sitting in the dentist's chair and being numbed, for example, without anxiety.

What Is the Difference between Sensitization and Desensitization?

While I was growing up on the farm, my family had a yearly tradition. On the last day of school, Mother would pick us up and take us to our favorite restaurant for lunch. After eating, we'd go home and plant our summer garden.

Each year, Mother gave me a special section of the garden to plant any type of flowers I liked. I loved to plant and tend bright red gladiolas, vibrant yellow roses, and shocking pink snapdragons. I was involved in 4-H and won several best-of-show awards for gardening.

Mother's interest in the garden was different from mine. She loved fresh vegetables, and by springtime each year she yearned for the taste of fresh corn on the cob. She planted corn every June with the anticipation of eating her mouth-watering harvest in September. However, she was disappointed every year. One year a group of pheasants got into her garden and ate the crop. The next summer, she put up a pathetic-looking scarecrow, which did nothing to deter the birds that pecked the ears of corn to mere cobs. The following year, a deer jumped over the tall fence into the garden. And another year, we had an early frost that destroyed the corn before it could ripen.

Despite the obstacles, Mother didn't give up on her dream of homegrown corn. As a last-ditch effort, she decided to give her corn a head start and planted the seeds in small pots late in April. By the time June came and the weather warmed up, she would be able to transplant her tender seedlings directly into the fresh earth.

On the last day of school that year, she could hardly finish her lunch; she was so excited to plant her young corn plants. She had taken good care of them and they were about eight inches tall.

That afternoon, I proposed a contest. I planted corn seeds, and Mother planted her seedlings. We were both sure our own plants would produce first, but which one of us do you think harvested corn that year?

Let's just say Mother was a gracious loser. Why didn't her plants yield a harvest? Mother's plants were not climatized or desensitized to the cold, rainy June we had in the Pacific Northwest. Mother's plants were "sensitized" to the indoor air and soil. Coming from the warm house, it took time for the young corn plants to become "desensitized" to the colder, wetter outdoor conditions. It took them six weeks to catch up with the seeds I planted directly into the soil. Their desensitization took time.

I've learned a valuable lesson from my plants that I now apply to my counseling. God has a timetable for growth. Just as I couldn't put the seeds in the ground and hope to have corn or flowers in my garden the next morning, neither can a person with an anxiety disorder expect it to go away within a day or two. Many people who come to me in my counseling practice want a pill to make their anxieties instantly disappear. Although medication can help in many cases, it can't do everything. You must be willing to invest the time and effort required to move toward healing and wholeness.

What Are the Steps Involved in Desensitization?

One of the ways I remember Mother expressing her love to Father was when she baked him a batch of his favorite cookies. His eyes sparkled with adoration when he enjoyed her delicious cookies and a hot cup of coffee. Wanting the same attention from Father, I asked Mother to teach me to bake like she did. Our first project was a batch of chocolate-chip cookies.

Before she let me do anything on my own, Mother made me watch her mix the batter, spoon it onto the pan, and bake it. The next time, she explained how to read the recipe and measure the ingredients correctly. Then she watched me as I mixed and stirred the batter. Finally, on our third batch, I got to do the entire task by myself, though still under Mother's watchful eye. Those cookies were the best I'd ever tasted!

One day when she wasn't home, I decided I was ready to go solo. I couldn't wait to see my father's face when I presented him with what I was sure would be the most delicious cookies he had ever tasted. Unfortunately, I put too much flour into the batter and the cookies came out of the oven as hard as rocks.

Being the loving and gracious parents they were, Father smiled his beautiful smile of love and approval, and Mother kindly told me that she liked the cookies because she could dunk them in her coffee. She didn't want me to feel as if I was a failure for trying to venture out on my own. I am thankful that she gave me the freedom to try, because when I finally learned to make them, my family raved about how delicious they were—and they meant it! Success was sweet that day!

Just like learning to bake cookies, systematic desensitization is a slow process of watching and then doing what is necessary to expose your anxieties. The following nine-step process will give you a quick overview on what it takes to desensitize yourself to your anxieties.

1. **Acknowledge your anxieties.** Admitting your anxieties takes courage. It isn't easy, but it's the first step in overcoming them. Try writing out your anxieties. Make a list of the activities or relationships you've missed out on because of them.

2. **Focus your energy on one source of anxiety.** Don't try to conquer all your anxieties at once. Start with one and gain victory with it before moving on to the next. Success builds on success.

3. **Ask a counselor, spouse, or friend to help you.** Scripture states, "Two are better than one because they have a good return for their work" (Ecclesiastes 4:9). A therapist can best help you deal with anxiety that is significantly impairing your life. A spouse or friend can go with you as you drive over that bridge for the first time, look at a snake in the zoo, or attend a social event with strangers.

4. **Develop a plan.** Your therapist will talk with you about how to overcome your anxiousness, and then together you can write out a specific treatment plan. An old proverb says, "The journey of a thousand miles begins with a single step." You know what the desired outcome is; now lay out the steps you will have to take to get there.

5. **Relax and visualize yourself doing what you fear.** When you are in a relaxed state, think about successfully approaching or doing what

you fear. In time, you will associate feeling relaxed with flying, swimming, or sitting in a dentist's chair.

6. **Expose yourself to your anxiety in small increments.** If you're afraid of spiders, you don't need to run out and buy a pet tarantula. Just take one step at a time. Perhaps you could start by trying not to take a wide path around a spider you see on the sidewalk. Next time you see one, stop and observe it. Try to relax as you watch this fascinating member of God's creation. Don't rush yourself, but try to keep making progress.

7. **Repeat the activity on your own.** When you've experienced success with a friend, take the next step by yourself.

8. **Treat yourself to a reward.** When you've reached your goal, celebrate! If you've overcome a fear of flying, buy a new piece of luggage (or if you're on a budget, a new luggage tag!). Include the friend who gave you a helping hand and thank that person for being a part of your healing.

9. **Persevere in tackling your anxiety.** Once you've rewarded yourself, proceed to the next phobia or anxiety. Facing down your anxiety will get easier with practice and time. Be willing to put up with momentary discomfort to accomplish your long-term goals.

As Christians, we have a solid basis for optimism and hope. Remember the poetic imagery of Deuteronomy 33:26-27a: "There is no one like the God of Jeshurun, who rides on the heavens to help you and on the clouds in his majesty. The eternal God is your refuge, and underneath are the everlasting arms."

Underneath you are the everlasting arms of God's loving support. When you take gradual steps to diminish your anxieties, he is by your side every step of the way. Form a mental picture of the two of you—with the support of others in the body of Christ—making progress together.

Power Tools

Systematic desensitization is a tool that will yield results. If you follow the steps above, you can learn to manage your anxiety. Your opportunities for new experiences and relationships no longer need to be limited by your fears.

Power Padlock: My anxieties have caused me to miss out on so much in my life already. It's just too late to start over.

Power Principle: It's never too late to make positive change in your life. Reducing your anxieties will open up opportunities for you in ways you've not yet imagined.

Power Passage: "Restore us to yourself, O LORD, that we may return; renew our days as of old" (Lamentations 5:21).

Power Question: Why do I let my anxiety control me instead of controlling my anxiety so I can live a full life?

Power Padlock: I have so many phobias. I'll never overcome them; it's hopeless.

Power Principle: Tackle your phobias or anxieties individually. You can overcome each of them one step at a time.

Power Passage: "Not only so, but we also rejoice in our sufferings, because we know that suffering produces perseverance; perseverance, character; and character, hope. And hope does not disappoint us, because God has poured out his love into our hearts by the Holy Spirit, whom he has given us" (Romans 5:3–5).

Power Question: What steps can I take this week to begin the process of desensitization?

Power Padlock: I can't even imagine being free from the bondage of anxiety.

Power Principle: God is not limited by what we can imagine or hope for.

Power Passage: "Now to him who is able to do immeasurably more than all we ask or imagine, according to his power that is at work within us, to him be glory ... for ever and ever!" (Ephesians 3:20–21).

Power Question: How would my life be different if I learned to manage my anxiety?

Power Padlock: This is too much work. It's easier to just stay bound by my anxiety.

Power Principle: Growth and change take time and work. If you want to be free, you need to persevere.

Power Passage: "... let us throw off everything that hinders and the sin that so easily entangles, and let us run with perseverance the race marked out for us" (Hebrews 12:1).

Power Question: What holds me back from trusting God to move forward in taking control of my physical response to anxiety?

The decision to use medication is an individual one between patient and medical doctor or psychiatrist. The following list is only a few of the most common reasons to consider medications; there are many others. Please consult your health care provider for the advantages and disadvantages of medication in your individual case.

Medical doctor's or psychiatrist's recommendation

Experiencing moderate to severe anxiety symptoms with little or no improvement

Daily practicing deep breathing and other relaxation techniques for 6–8 weeks with no marked difference

Impairment of your life by an inability to go to work and function as a "normal" adult

Change of behavior that is harmful to self or others

A family history of anxiety disorders or suicide

Thoughts of your own self-harm, suicidal ideation, or a past suicide attempt

Inability to sleep or eat normal meals

Out-of-control feelings that cause you to quickly become agitated, angry, or violent

Naming symptoms of OCD, severe Panic Disorder, or acute PTSD

10 Medications:
Prescribed by Professionals

"I've always prided myself on my good health," Mike informs the group. "I've never had anything wrong with me—I've never needed to take medication for anything—and I don't plan to start now!"

Mike tells the therapy group about some of his combat experiences in Vietnam. "I put my life on the line for this country every day—I had an important job to do—I didn't have time to feel sorry for myself." Mike continues to brag about the importance of his wartime accomplishments. "Vietnam taught me that real men are strong, and weakness is not to be tolerated under any circumstance.

"Taking medication is for weaklings only. I know I don't need it. My medical doctor and now my new psychiatrist think I need medication to manage my life. My marriage and job might be in a slump right now, but I know I can handle it."

Debbie turns to address Mike. "Mike, you're going to be a very unhappy man until you learn to express your anger. You're going to lose many important things in your life if you don't work on managing your anxiety."

Mike looks directly into Debbie's soft turquoise eyes. Her baby blues remind him of his mother. He realizes she has the same petite build as his mother had many years ago. A horrible memory flashes again across the screen of his mind: His mother had left him with a babysitter who molested him. *I hate her! I'll never forgive her!* he finds himself thinking.

Mike's mind returns to the present and he directs his pent-up frustration toward Debbie. "I've tried deep breathing for two months—I've tried all *your* stretching and muscle exercises—I've tried *your* meditation and prayer—and nothing *you've* suggested works for me."

Debbie notices the edge emerging in Mike's words.

Mike pauses for a moment and adds in a louder voice, "If I don't get those flashbacks to stop, I'll lose my wife—I'll lose my job—and I'll lose my beautiful children. I don't have time to play games with you or to wait for that so-called 'miracle' medication to start doing its job." With those words, Mike's face flushes with rage. He looks at Debbie and confronts her again: "You're just like my mother."

Debbie perceives Mike's statements as his attempt to transfer his pain from his mother to her so she listens with great empathy.

"You say you want to help, but when it comes down to it, you really don't care about me. You're just like her!" He swears under his breath while describing his mother's not-so-flattering qualities. "She was too busy with her boyfriends to realize that I was being molested when she left me with the babysitter."

Mike's behavior spins out of control as he shouts profanities and moves toward the window where there is an extra chair. He picks up the chair and looks at Debbie. His body shakes with the intensity of his fury. He shouts, "I hate you! You're just like all the other women in my life. Every one of them has let me down!"

"Stop it right there!" Debbie commands Mike. "Put that chair down! Get control of yourself and sit down right now. I will not allow you to harm yourself or anyone else." Debbie enforces firm boundaries with Mike to deescalate his behavior before it gets further out of control.

"If you break that window," Debbie continues, "you'll pay for it. I care enough about you to not let you harm yourself or anyone else. I'll not hesitate to call the police to protect everyone in this room. They'll take you to jail or to a psychiatric hospital for evaluation." She looks at the group members. Their faces have turned white with fear. She knows she has a tense situation on her hands that requires all her expertise as a therapist.

Mike's mind momentarily shifts to the past. He vividly recalls an experience his Vietnam buddy related to him. His friend had been confined to a small cell for several months. One by one, fellow Americans in surrounding cells had been tortured and killed. The possibility of captivity sends Mike's mind spiraling into a dark world in his past.

It is the sound of a car backfiring in a parking lot near Debbie's office that brings his mind back to the present. He realizes he is out of control and quickly puts down the chair. "Dear God, what have I become?"

"Mike," Debbie instructs, "take some deep breaths to relax your body."

Mike sighs, thinking a little further, and concludes, "No wonder my wife and mother are so afraid of me. I'm a monster, and I'm scared of myself. I'm not going to behave like this anymore," Mike tells Debbie as he regains control of his emotions.

He points at Debbie. "How could you let me get like this? You were supposed to take care of me. You're just like my mother. She never protected me from the babysitter, either. That girl molested me when I was too young to fight back. No one defended me. I'm angry that you, just like she, didn't do more to help me."

Debbie pauses for a few moments to let Mike calm down and think about the situation that has transpired. Her mind drifts back to her internship. She learned a critical lesson from her clinical supervisor at that time. He helped her learn not to take her patients' anger personally. He encouraged her to instead use it as an opportunity to help her patients grow and learn to process feelings.

"I know you're angry with me," Debbie tells Mike, "but will you let me help you keep from harming yourself or others? I *do* care about you, and it means a lot to me that you felt comfortable in sharing your emotions with me. Will you let me help you with your anger toward your mother?"

Mike slowly nods.

"I'm encouraged with your progress," Debbie explains. "Many people diagnosed with PTSD say their emotions are 'frozen in time.' As you recover, there will be a 'thawing' of your emotions and thinking that will reflect a major step in your healing. It's possible that medication could help you stabilize your body so that you can more effectively access your emotions and thinking."

"But I don't want to take medication," Mike reminds Debbie.

"I respect your right to have choices," Debbie replies. "I don't understand why you wouldn't want to take it if your psychiatrist and your medical doctor think it would help."

"It is considered 'unspiritual' in my church. An elder told me my flashbacks would stop if I would just read my Bible and go to church more often. A friend of my wife's thinks I'm demon-possessed."

"Medication is a tool God has given us to help people," Debbie explains. "If you had heart disease, would it be a sin to use medication? What if you had diabetes and needed insulin? Would that be a sign of spiritual weakness? Wouldn't it be a poor decision not to take the medication and risk dying?"

"Well, yes," Mike answers hesitantly, "but this is different."

"How's that?"

"Because a mental disorder is a weakness," Mike tells her "It's because of a lack of faith!"

"That doesn't make sense," Debbie answers Mike. "People who struggle with PTSD were casualties of natural disasters, war, or violent crimes. They didn't do *anything* to cause their pain. They are victims of unfortunate circumstances and other people's sin."

"I'm still not convinced," Mike responds.

Debbie pauses, then looks intently at him. "Do you mean to tell me that God would say that when you were abused by the babysitter as a three-year-old child you were responsible? Do you really believe that God holds you accountable for that person's sin?"

"Well, I guess you've got a point," Mike acknowledges.

"Mike, you've been through some terrible things," Debbie reassures him. "That doesn't make you bad, but you do need some help. The situation today highlights that something must be done before you further hurt yourself or someone else."

Mike asks Debbie, "Could you spend some time during this session talking more about medication?"

"I can't tell you which ones to take," Debbie admits, "but I can give you some educational information about medication that will help you understand what your doctor or psychiatrist is recommending."

Debbie proceeds to share with the group the advantages and disadvantages of using medication to treat anxiety. She emphasizes that before taking any medication each individual needs to consult a licensed medical professional.

Why Not Use Medication?

Deep breathing, relaxation techniques, meditation, self-talk, and systematic desensitization can all be used with or without medications. These "natural alternatives" work particularly well for people with mild to moderate cases of anxiety. (However, there are some moderate to severe cases of anxiety like Obsessive Compulsive Disorder that are most likely genetic and require medication to stabilize.)

There are some situations in which medication is generally not used:

- People who have specific allergies must avoid certain classifications of medications. (Be sure to inform your doctor of allergies you have.)

- People who are recovering from substance abuse and other addictions are generally not prescribed any medications that could be habit forming and addictive, such as Benzodiazepines.

- People with certain physical health conditions find that some types of medications can create additional problems. For example, Benzodiazepines can affect the balance of an elderly person who already struggles to stay steady on his feet.

- People with diabetes, or liver, kidney, or heart concerns may be limited in their choice of anti-anxiety medications.

- People with certain mental health diagnoses, such as characterological issues—borderline, histrionic, narcissistic, and so forth—require long-term therapy, and medication is not of value. If there is a corresponding anxiety or other mental health diagnosis, however, medication could be helpful.

- A person's physician may decide that it is in the patient's best interest not to use medication.

- People who choose to continue using alcohol or other drugs should not take anti-anxiety medication. These substances can reduce the positive effects of the medication, can increase addiction issues, and with Benzodiazepine can lead to life-threatening situations.

There are many other possible reasons not to use medication. In many other cases medication could be helpful. Please consult with your physician or psychiatrist to address your individual situation.

Why Use Medication?

- Medication may be used when there is a change in sleep patterns, appetite, or energy level, which is a physiological indicator of impairment.

- Medication may be used in cases where deep breathing, relaxation techniques, meditation, and self-talk have been utilized for a prolonged period without any significant reduction in symptoms.

- Medication is used in an acute mental health crisis—when a person goes to the ER thinking he's having a heart attack—to stabilize an individual's condition.

- Medication is used so a person can participate in therapy when a crisis threatens the structure and stability of an individual's family system. For example, when a mother with severe Obsessive Compulsive Disorder neglects her children in favor of her rituals, medication could be used to disengage her from those rituals and help her connect with her children.

- Medication may be used in moderate to severe cases of anxiety, such as Obsessive Compulsive Disorder, which are most likely genetic.

- Medication may be used to enhance and sometimes shorten treatment.

- Medication may be used when an individual's life is significantly impaired by anxiety. For example, the person can't hold down a job, take care of small children, or have adequate social relationships.

- Medication is used to help a person address significant issues in therapy that they might not otherwise be able to uncover, including problems in daily functioning. For example, a person who, because of a social phobia, can't begin the process of desensitization, may be able to enter a crowded room for the first time with an initial dose of medication.

- Medication may help in an acute mental crisis when a person wants to harm himself (suicidal) or someone else (homicidal) or commit a violent act against another.

The decision to use medication is an individual one between a patient and his medical doctor or psychiatrist. I don't force my clients to use medication, but in most cases, I present it as an option. I do refer them to licensed professionals to evaluate their cases to determine if medication would be helpful. These professionals are responsible for helping the patients and their families weigh the advantages and disadvantages of medication.

I also encourage my patients to include family members or other significant people in their initial medication evaluation ("med. eval."). Each patient however, must ultimately make his individual choice. Some people want to avoid medication and are willing to invest the time and attention needed to manage their anxiety without it. Others have reached a point of desperation and are willing to try medication as an alternative.

If a person chooses to try to reduce anxiety for a short period either with or without medication, I let him know that he will have to make significant lifestyle changes. He will need to

- Create a daily schedule that encourages extra time for deep breathing and other relaxation techniques;
- Change his routine to include daily prayer or meditation;
- Commit himself to a regular program of exercise and balanced diet;
- Construct a plan for changing his thoughts, self-talk, and view of life;
- Create a good support system with friends and family where he can pour out his heart;
- Consider a less driven approach to life;
- Confront fear or anxiety issues underlying his disorder in long-term therapy;
- Connect his anxiety issues to other issues within his family and seek treatment accordingly.

What Are the Different Kinds of Anti-Anxiety Medications?

There are five different types of medications used for treating anxiety disorders. (Many of these medications are also used to treat depression. A majority of the people diagnosed with an anxiety disorder are also diagnosed with depression.) We will discuss the advantages and disadvantages of each category of medication.

Category #1—SSRI Antidepressant Medications

In the past few years, SSRIs (selective serotonin reuptake inhibitors) have become the most popular medications used by most psychiatrists and medical doctors to treat anxiety disorders and depression.

SSRIs are used most frequently for Generalized Anxiety Disorder, Panic Disorder with or without a history of agoraphobia, Obsessive Compulsive Disorder, Social Phobia, and sometimes PTSD. Included in this popular antidepressant category are Prozac, Zoloft, Paxil, Luvox, Serzone, and Celexa.

What are the advantages to SSRIs?

The primary reason SSRIs have become so widely used is their limited side effects.

SSRIs tend to be more effective than traditional antidepressants and can be used for the chronically medically ill or elderly because these medications are more specifically targeted to the underlying chemistry of anxiety and depression.

What are the disadvantages to SSRIs?

To achieve maximum benefits from an SSRI, you'll need to take it for nine to twelve months or as long as your doctor prescribes, which can get expensive. At the time of the writing of this book, it is possible that an uninsured person could pay several hundred dollars per month for some SSRIs. Those who do not complete their medication course risk having to return to treatment. It creates less expense and hassle for them in the long run to stay on the medication. Most SSRIs are protected by patents, and there aren't yet many generic SSRIs. In the future, cost should be less of an issue after the patent protection expires. The newer more expensive SSRIs specifically target the chemistry of anxiety and depression.

In the beginning, some of those who take SSRIs will experience jitteriness, agitation, restlessness, dizziness, drowsiness, headaches, nausea, gastrointestinal distress, and sexual dysfunction. These side effects generally subside in two weeks. Lower dosages are often used to start the medication and increase over time until they reach therapeutic levels.

SSRIs have been known to sometimes trigger a manic episode for persons with bipolar disorder. SSRIs should only be used under the direction of a licensed physician or psychiatrist.

Category #2—Benzodiazepines

Benzodiazepines (BZs) are high-potency, fast-acting tranquilizers. Xanax, Ativan, and Klonopin are commonly used to treat severe anxiety disorders. Valium, Librium, or Tranxene may also be used but are often not preferred.

The differences in these medications have to do with how strong they are and how fast they act. The stronger the initial tranquilizer, the shorter it lasts, and the more addictive it becomes. For instance, Valium is a fast-acting tranquilizer and extremely addictive, whereas Klonopin lasts longer and is not as addictive.

Because these medications tend to be addictive, they are generally used more for severe, short-term anxiety issues.

Posttraumatic Stress Disorder and Obsessive Compulsive Disorder are generally better treated with antidepressants and SSRIs.

What are the advantages of BZs?

BZs generally work quickly, within 15–20 minutes. Unlike SSRIs, they can be taken on an "as needed" basis. You can take a dosage to confront a difficult situation like a job interview or a public speaking situation where you know you are going to be anxious.

BZs tend to have fewer side effects than antidepressant medications and can be more affordable, since generic forms of BZ are available. Other medications change the chemistry of the body; BZs tranquilize it.

What are the disadvantages of BZs?

Unlike other anti-anxiety medications, BZs tend to be addictive. The higher the dosage, the longer you take it, the more likely you are to become dependent. Abruptly stopping these medications can be dangerous, because it can produce panic attacks, severe anxiety, confusion, muscle tension, irritability, insomnia, seizures, and even death.

It is usually better to taper off these medications slowly. Don't "just stop" taking these medications. Don't take just one more because you think it will make you better. If you do, you may trigger a relapse with symptoms that can be greater than the original ones. BZs are the most highly addictive chemical substances known to man. If you take these medications for more than six to eight weeks, taper slowly. It is essential for you to follow your doctor's direction when taking these medications.

Another problem with BZs is that they can have an impact on your emotions. Many people who've used BZs report a "blunting effect" or a "muting effect" not only on their anxiety, but also on their feelings. BZs are a depressant. They depress the central nervous system. Often when a person has anxiety combined with depression, the depression can worsen, particularly with elderly persons. These people may have difficulty crying or expressing anger or other emotions in appropriate ways.

Although it is rare, some individuals may have what are called "paradoxical reactions" to BZs. This means that they become more violent, more impulsive, or more emotional when stopping the medication.

If people use BZs for more than two years, they tend to complain that the medication "zaps" them of their energy. Don't forget that BZs are tranquilizers, and they are designed to have sedating effect, which causes drowsiness and fatigue. It should come as no surprise that people can become more depressed and less energetic the longer they take this medication. This is a drawback because people tend to rely on medication instead of learning to control their bodies.

BZs can cause difficulty in breathing, driving, or operating heavy machinery. BZs can affect the liver, so liver tests are sometimes performed on people over fifty.

BZs are generally used initially for treating short-term, acute anxiety. In the long term, people are usually transferred to SSRIs. BZs are not usually used for long-term anxiety issues such as agoraphobia with Panic, Posttraumatic Stress Disorder or Obsessive Compulsive Disorder.

Category #3—Tricyclic Antidepressants

Tryclcylic antidepressants include Tofranil (imipramine), Pamelor (nortriptyline), Norpramin (desipramine), Anafranil (clomipramine), Elavil (amitriptyline), Desyrel (trazadone), Sinequan (doxepin), and others. They are not used as often as other anti-anxiety medications because they have more side effects. It is usually best to start these medications slowly and work up to therapeutic levels. Certain tricyclic antidepressant medications are used to treat Panic Disorder either with or without a history of agoraphobia, and others are used for OCD.

What are the advantages to tricyclic antidepressant medications?

An advantage of the tricyclics is that they don't lead to physical dependence. In addition, there are generic forms of these medications available, making them more affordable.

What are the disadvantages to tricyclic antidepressant medications?

One disadvantage of this class of medication is their side effects. Unlike SSRIs, they tend to produce dry mouth, blurred vision, dizziness or disorientation, and postural hypotension (lightheadedness and dizziness), sedation, and constipation. In addition, the side affects of weight gain and sexual dysfunction can also create problems that the patient must cope with.

Although many side effects tend to subside after a week or two, they are not eliminated in 25 to 30 percent of the people.

Category #4—MAO Inhibitors

Nardil (pheneleine) and Parnate (tranylcypromine) are two medications used in this class. Considered the oldest class of antidepressant medications, MAO Inhibitors are not often prescribed. They are generally used in treating Social Phobia and Panic Disorder. You should be in close contact with your doctor if you're taking one of these.

What are the advantages and disadvantages of MAOIs?

The main advantage to MAOIs is they can be used as an alternative when other medications haven't worked. However, one major concern with MAOIs is sudden and even fatal changes in blood pressure. If you take this medication, ask your doctor which foods to avoid.

Other side effects of MAOIs are weight gain, sexual dysfunction, headache, fatigue, and insomnia. These may increase during the third or fourth week of treatment but are likely to diminish.

Dietary restrictions are critical. You'll need to avoid certain foods, over the counter diet pills, antihistamines, SSRIs, or tricyclic antidepressants.

Category #5—Beta-Blockers

The most common forms of beta-blockers are Interal (propranolol) and Tenormin (etenolol). These medications are also used to treat heart and other medical problems. For people with anxiety, beta-blockers help reduce heart palpitations, blushing, and sweating.

What are the advantages of beta-blockers?

Beta-blockers can be used in single dosages to reduce anxiety symptoms in overwhelming situations for people with Social Phobia. Sometimes a single dosage is given to people who experience a surge of anxiety when they present a speech, go for a job interview, or perform at a musical recital.

What are the disadvantages of beta-blockers?

Beta-blockers can lower blood pressure (resulting in dizziness or lightheadedness) and cause drowsiness or fatigue. They are not recommended for people with diabetes, asthma, or respiratory illness that causes wheezing. It is generally recommended that you taper these medications slowly to avoid a sudden change in blood pressure.

Category #6—BuSpar

BuSpar is most often used for the treatment of Generalized Anxiety Disorder and Social Phobia, but generally has little impact on the length or frequency of Panic.

The advantage of BuSpar is that it is less likely to cause drowsiness and it is non-addictive. There is little risk at becoming dependent on it, but some do report feeling lethargy, nausea, dizziness, or paradoxical anxiety.

Category #7—Other Medications

When other medications fail, sometimes Depakote (valproic acid) or Neurontin (gabapentin) are used to treat anxiety. They were originally used for seizures and have also been used for mood disorders such as bipolar.

In addition, there is a final group of antidepressants used to fight anxiety that does not have a specific name. One of these medications is Effexor (venlafaxine) that combines an SSRI and a tricyclic antidepressant in one pill. It is helpful for those with Obsessive Compulsive Disorder and depression. Remeron (mirtazepine) is a newer medication.

Wellbutrin (bupropion) is used for depression but can be difficult for some people with anxiety disorders to tolerate as it can further increase anxiety.

Will Medication Solve All My Problems?

Medication works differently in each person. Consider the idea that you and your doctor are solving a puzzle together. You may need to try different dosages of different kinds of medications before the pieces of the puzzle come together. Don't just take a single dosage or type of medication, decide it's not working, and give up. Certain categories of medications must be taken for a length of time to be effective.

Some people view medication as a quick fix or an easy answer. Medication is *not* a cure-all for all anxiety disorders. People with anxiety problems still need to manage their anxiety in long-term therapy. Medication may reduce the length of treatment, but patients will still have to learn to manage their anxiety.

Why Don't People Take Responsibility to Help Themselves?

As a therapist, I encourage my patients to take adult responsibility for managing their anxiety. When I was a zealous young youth worker in my early twenties, I learned an important lesson that I've carried into my counseling practice.

There was a student in my youth ministry whose family—his widowed mother and two sisters—needed help moving. The four of them had an opportunity to move from an old apartment in a bad part of town to low-income housing in another part of town.

I gathered the students from our group together and encouraged them to help the family with an old-fashioned moving party. The students were enthused and felt it was a way of demonstrating Christian love and charity to others. Some of the girls gathered boxes from a grocery store. Another student was able to secure the use of his father's truck for this venture.

When I entered the family home, I was overtaken by the poverty. I was determined not to let the students know how repulsed I was by the filth and stench that had overwhelmed me. I had compassion on the family because I knew the father's death had taken most of their limited financial resources.

As my eyes scanned the apartment, I couldn't find anything of material value. The most valuable thing seemed to be an old black-and-white television. I wanted to protect their one "nice" item from being scratched in the move, and so I asked the family for a blanket.

The mother and son looked at each other and didn't seem to know what to do. The mother rushed into her makeshift bedroom and reappeared with a tattered, stained relic of a blanket. When I unfolded it, I saw that it was more hole than blanket. My heart broke when I realized this family didn't have a blanket. Later, I cried when I realized I had offended this poverty-stricken family.

Several days later, I wanted to make up for my mistake. I called friends at church to help me gather used blankets, bedding, towels, and canned food. That Sunday after church, I left the items on their front porch. When I got to my office on Monday morning, I received a telephone call from the student's mother. She didn't appreciate my "charity."

From this experience, I learned a valuable lesson about helping others. I wanted to help them, but in my ignorance I brought further pain to this family.

You can't help others until they're ready for your help. Until they are willing to acknowledge their need and reach out, no one can help them. In the zeal of my youth, I attempted to help people who didn't want my help. As a therapist, I don't push people to take medication or even to get well. I've learned to hear "no" from my patients and not own their responsibility to make their own healthy choices.

Those who struggle with pride in relationship to taking medication are often unwilling to accept help from a medical professional. These people may be missing an opportunity to utilize a tool for healing and wellness. Ultimately, each person must decide if he or she wants help or not. I do encourage my patients to discuss medication with a psychiatrist or medical doctor, gathering as much information as they need in order to make an informed decision.

Is Medication All There Is?

Debbie referred Mike to a psychiatrist to evaluate if medication could be used in his specific case. She set limits on his behavior to protect both him and others from physical harm. She respected his right to take adult authority to make choices about the stewardship of his body. She didn't manipulate or strong-arm him, but waited patiently for him to see his needs. In the end, he did finally agree to take medication.

Before I went back to school and completed my master's degree, I worked in three different in-patient psychiatric hospitals in preparation for becoming a mental-health therapist. One of the things that quickly amazed me was the difference medication made in the lives of my patients. I couldn't believe how quickly some people with severe conditions improved. I remember leaving work on the weekends, and when I returned on Monday mornings, I found patients who often had made remarkable improvements.

I realized, though, that medication was not the total answer; it was only the first step in the healing process. Behavior changes—supported by long-term, consistent therapy—were needed as well.

It takes a mature person to acknowledge they have a need and then seek the necessary help to meet that need. Medication is not always the answer for everyone, but in some cases it is a step that, when combined with intense therapy, can make a tremendous difference.

Until Mike had the crisis, he didn't realize how much his behavior impacted others. It took losing control of his temper coupled with the possibility of jail or further hospitalization to cause him to return to his senses. Debbie did the most loving thing possible by allowing him to work through his anger with her about his medication and his mother.

When group members prepare to discharge, some are elated and some are frightened. Many will have been with the group for six months to a year. During the recovery process, the group has become a "safe harbor" for the wounded as they navigate through some of the intense storms of life. The structure has helped to create a sense of security and stability.

When patients enter the group, their first task is to leave the darkness of their isolation and join the warmth and light of the group. Many are so fearful and hurt that they have to relearn the process of relating to and trusting others.

As discharge approaches, the therapist will help them begin the process of disconnecting or "detaching" from the group and reconnecting or "attaching" with supportive people in their church and community.

It is not uncommon for people with anxiety disorders to fear discharge. As they get closer to it, they sometimes feel they are regressing. This is seldom true. The therapist will reassure the patient that his feelings are normal, but he is indeed progressing and no longer needs this level of treatment.

Even with this reassurance, there are those who will attempt to sabotage treatment by becoming helpless and fearful as the structure of the group dissolves.

The therapist's goal is to either help them build a new network of support, or, if one is already in place, to transition them back to their respective spiritual and social communities.

Wonderful things can happen when we choose to consider what's available to assist us in our journey to freedom from anxiety. The medications that you are too embarrassed to consider or too ashamed to admit you might need can actually be valuable allies in a successful strategy to beat anxiety disorders.

Paul says in Romans 8:37 that we are more than conquerors through the power of God's love. Conquerors never enter battle without their armor, their troops, their weapons, and their battle plan. It may be that medication is a piece of battle gear that will allow you to turn the tide of battle in your favor.

Power Tools

God created each of us with the ability to make choices. He isn't a giant puppeteer in heaven who moves a string and forces us to raise our arms or legs. He loves us enough to give us choices about what we will do with our lives.

Love never blossoms in an environment of control or fear. It grows when those who love us give us the freedom to make choices. To recover, we need to be in loving relationship with people who will hold us accountable and still allow us to take responsibility for our lives.

Power Padlock: Why do others want to tell me what to do with my body?

Power Principle: God expects us to make informed choices with the assistance of licensed professionals about medication and other treatment issues regarding my anxiety.

Power Promise: "… Choose for yourselves this day whom you will serve …" (Joshua 24:15).

Power Question: Why do I resist taking adult responsibility for the stewardship of my life? Why is it easier to rely upon someone else?

Power Padlock: I don't want to put the effort into managing my anxiety; it is my body and I can do anything I please with it.

Power Principle: God intends for us to take adult responsibility for making choices that impact our bodies. We are responsible to ask informed questions about anxiety and work at managing it.

Power Promise: "Do you not know that your body is a temple of the Holy Spirit, who is in you, whom you have received from God? You are not your own; you were bought with a price, therefore honor God with your body" (1 Corinthians 6:19–20).

Power Question: What can I do to take responsibility to manage my body?

Power Padlock: Why do I have to work at managing my anxiety?

Power Principle: I will have to take responsibility to control my anxiety.

Power Promise: "But the fruit of the Spirit is love, joy, peace, patience, kindness, goodness, faithfulness, gentleness and self-control" (Galatians 5:22–23).

Power Question: What is one thing I can do today to start becoming responsible for the management of my anxiety?

Power Padlock: I don't have any choices regarding the treatment of my anxiety.

Power Principle: You can't accept God's love without understanding that he loves us enough to give us free-will or choices.

Power Promise: "It is for freedom that Christ has set us free" (Galatians 5:1).

Power Question: How can I make good choices about my anxiety today that help to demonstrate God's love?

Part 3 Unleashing the Power of Community

"We have all known the long loneliness and we have learned that the only solution is love and that love comes with community."
—Dorothy Day

Note: Many people complain that they don't know where to go to find new relationships. Listed below are a few ideas to get you started.

Risk getting involved with your community, city government, or public school system.

Exercise or join a swim, aerobics, hiking, or walking club.

Learn a new skill by taking a community college course.

Attend a Bible study or a men's or women's fellowship group.

Take a painting, music, woodworking, or craft class.

Invite someone to coffee or lunch following a church event.

Organize a prayer group, Bible study, or mother's support group.

Notice new people who come into your life and introduce yourself to them.

Serve on a church committee.

Help at a hospital, youth center, or nursing home.

Invest your skills in helping others through teaching, coaching, or speaking.

Partner with others to do volunteer work.

11 Your Need for Relationship:
Learning to Trust Others Again

"W-w-what do you mean, I need to have 'people' to recover from my anxiety disorder?" Steve asks Debbie.

"Its a biblical concept," Debbie explains to Steve, "we need to be in relationship to heal. The Scriptures give us an important principle that supports this idea: "Two are better than one. ... If one falls down his friend can help him up. But pity the man who falls down and has none to pick him up" (Ecclesiastes 4:9–10).

Debbie turns to the other group members and continues to explain the importance of this principle. "As we are journeying on the road of life, sometimes our hearts will be bruised and damaged. God brings people into our lives to help pick us up emotionally and 'safeguard' our continued growth.

"One of my favorite Bible stories is about a man who was emotionally and physically hurt (see Mark 2:1–5). This man was a paraplegic who'd been paralyzed since birth. One day, his friends brought him to Jesus on a stretcher. Swarms flocked to hear Jesus speak, and the four men couldn't get through to carry their friend into the room. The determined and creative men cut a hole in the roof and lowered the man into the room where Jesus was speaking. These men committed to responding to a friend's need. We need friends, like these men, who will hear our needs when we're in crisis and respond.

"Not all of us are fortunate enough to have friends as loyal as the paraplegic man's friends. God designed the body of Christ to serve as a healing agent to mend the broken and damaged parts of our hearts. He intended that we'd heal as we came into relationship. He intended that the inner turmoil, pain, confusion and fear that contribute to an anxiety disorder be healed as we establish a relationship with Him and with others in the body of Christ."

"Isn't it possible to recover on my own?" Steve questions Debbie. "Can't I just go into the woods and pray, sing praises, or memorize more Scripture?"

"It doesn't usually work like that," Debbie replies. "You and the other group members are preparing to discharge. If you don't strengthen your connections with others, you will sabotage your therapy."

"I-I-I hate to meet new people," Steve protests.

Debbie responds, "When we don't share our pain with others and we isolate instead, our anxiety tends to increase."

At this point Paula interjects, "I completely agree. I thought family was enough. I poured all my energy into raising my children. They left home, and now I have no one."

"Your experience is not uncommon, Paula, and its source goes all the way back to the original family," Debbie agrees. "When sin entered the world, all families became dysfunctional. God's plan is for the church to become the extended family and offer help and healing to those who are wounded."

Steve looks skeptical. "I've gone to church most of my life and heard many good sermons about love, but I've never heard that before. This relationship stuff is interesting."

"Can I ask you a question?" Debbie inquires, halting the interruptions and maintaining the structure of the group.

"I guess," Steve responds in an irritated tone. "You always say whatever you want to anyway."

"You sound a little frustrated, Steve. Is there something you'd like to say to me?"

"I don't want to hurt your feelings," Steve tells Debbie. "I like you, but I've got some issues with the way you do things."

"I want you to learn to share your feelings with me," Debbie encourages Steve. "That's how you'll get well. I want to remain 'safe' for you so you can process your frustration."

Steve takes a big breath before he continues. "I-I-I hate how you use these group rules about boundaries. I feel like I can't say anything without *you* correcting me. Sometimes it really bothers me that everything has to be so structured—you have to start the group *exactly* on time and end on time—you can't go one minute over time—I worry that if I'm a minute late and cross your boundaries, you'll make me look foolish to others in this group."

Debbie prompts Steve to process his feelings. "I appreciate that you are frustrated with me, but I think there's a deeper issue than just the structure of the group. I wonder if you might be fearful that, outside the group, others are not going to accept you. Are you already anticipating rejection? Is this possibility making you anxious?"

Steve blushes. "I get the point," he admits to Debbie. "Can we just go on? This is embarrassing."

"Of course," Debbie agrees, "though I hope we can return to it at some point. You always have the right to pass, and I'll respect you for telling me what you need." She clears her throat before she resuming her presentation.

"Let's get back to the concept of relationship. To further explain it, I'll tell you a story from my experience.

"One day I was scheduled to speak at a church conference on love and codependency. I ran home from a meeting with clients, changed my clothes, and jumped into my car, knowing I had just enough time to get there. When I started the car, however, I noticed, flashing on my dashboard, a red light with a picture of a gas tank. *What else?* I thought. *I can't be late. I can either stop now or stop on the interstate and wait for a police officer to stop and help.* I made the choice to stop driving and fill my tank at the gas station on the way.

"As I was filling my tank, I thought of an analogy that relates to what I've been trying to tell you. People with an anxiety disorder often go through life with empty emotional tanks. They struggle and hide because they are afraid of love. However, God designed relationships to be the emotional fuel we need to get through life. Without it, we will run out of the emotional energy we need to keep us functioning.

"As I continued to pump gas, my mind drifted back to my first car. One day my beloved car started to sputter. I took it to the mechanic and he told me I had used watered-down gas. He advised me to never use that brand of gas again because it was a cheap substitute. It looked like gas, but my engine knew the difference. It wouldn't run efficiently on inferior quality gas.

"Like my car, many of us have accepted an inferior form of emotional fuel." Debbie pauses as the group chuckles. "When we settle for inauthentic or unhealthy relationships, we deprive ourselves of the love and fellowship God intended us to have."

"Isn't fellowship just eating donuts and drinking coffee after church?" Paula asks.

"Not exactly," Debbie replies, "though donuts are a great picture of the heart of a person who has been hurt. That person's heart has a hole right in the middle that's never been filled by love. True fellowship means we share our deep pain, joy, and needs with others, and that's when the hole in the middle gets filled in!

"Though they didn't have coffee and donuts, Jesus ate his final meal with his disciples and shared the emotional pain of his impending betrayal and death.

"Even the Son of God needed relationship with others. Since we are created in God's image, we too are designed to need others."

"We are?" Steve inquires in a puzzled tone. "Why did He do that?"

"Because He loved us enough to want to be with us," Debbie assures Steve. "He created us with a need for relationship so we would seek to move toward Him and others."

How Do Relationships Help Those with Anxiety?

Relationships reduce anxiety when we are able to share with others our deepest pain. Anxiety that does not stem from a genetic issue is built on one or more of the following four specific categories of fear:

Fear of being close. This person fears abandonment and having his deepest pain revealed.

Fear of being separate. This person fears being alone, being enmeshed with, or engulfed by someone else.

Fear of shame, humiliation, and rejection when exposing one's weakness, "less-than-imperfect" or bad parts. The person fears exposing the weak or bad parts will erase or take away the good.

Fear of control. This person fears making decisions and being told what to do.

People with these fears need to share their feelings in the context of healthy relationships.

What Feelings Need to Be Shared?

At the root of the four categories of fear there are deep emotions we've often been afraid to share with others. Many of these relate to our insecurities about our weaknesses and struggles and manifest in a number of ways, including

- Fear of exposing needs
- Fear of being reliant on others
- Fear of abandonment
- Fear that others will let me down or disappointment me
- Fear of being unlovable
- Fear of betrayal
- Fear of rejection
- Fear of intimidation

- Fear of hearing or saying no
- Fear of rage
- Fear of further hurt, shame or humiliation
- Fear of becoming bitter
- Fear of showing anger or frustration
- Fear of feeling inferior
- Fear of disrespect

How Will I Learn to Share My Fear?

If you unveil your whole life to someone you don't know you are taking a risk. It's a little like giving a thief a blueprint to your house. You wouldn't tell the robber you are leaving the sliding glass door open and your diamond ring and pearls on the kitchen counter. That would be, as the Bible describes, "throwing your pearls before swine" (Matthew 7:6).

A smarter, safer way is to share your "pearls" slowly with other people until they've proven themselves worthy of your trust. If they can't keep your "pearls" to themselves, you certainly should exercise caution before sharing anything further.

People with an anxiety disorder need to find relationships where they can share their pain, embarrassment, shame, and distress with another person. This requires taking the time to establish those relationships.

In the initial stages of new relationships, you need "safer" people to share with. As you grow, you'll be able to share more with others. You'll become more comfortable with yourself and others, and you'll be better equipped to choose healthier relationships.

How Do You Get Started Finding Healthy People?

It takes an investment of time and effort to establish supportive relationships. I tell my patients that Alcoholics Anonymous has a great principle that people with anxiety disorders would do well to adopt. AA encourages new members who are recently sober to attend "ninety meetings in ninety days."

I encourage those recovering from an anxiety disorder to seek out ninety relational or "heart" contacts in ninety days. By adapting AA's idea, I hope to motivate others to understand the importance of establishing relationships. I ask my patients to open their hearts to receive love from another once each day. For the hurting and anxious person, this might seem like an impossible task. Using another AA slogan—one day at a time—helps them to get started by establishing a relational contact at least once a day.

In the Pacific Northwest, many of our leisure activities focus on the outdoors. I suggest my anxious patients walk their dogs in a park. I've found that some of them are able to use their pets as a way to initiate a conversation with other dog owners. I encourage others to make a phone call to a friend they've not seen in a while. Others may choose to go for a walk with a friend on the beach. At the beginning, the issue is the quantity of conversations, not the quality. As you learn to relate to others and begin to deepen your relationships by talking about more important matters, the quality will follow.

In college, my undergraduate work was in speech communications. My professors spent endless hours lecturing us on surface, close, intimate, and peak levels of communication. That information helped me to create a game plan for developing new relationships.

1. **Surface-level communication** is small talk about things that don't really matter. This level carries the least risk in talking with strangers. Examples of this are the weather, the traffic problem, or the location of the nearest coffee shop. At a social gathering, this is the most common form of communication.

2. **Close communication** emerges when we offer our opinions about politics, world events, or current affairs. It is a little more risky because it uncovers our values, likes, and dislikes. If I tell you I like bright colors, for example, it could let you know I like warm, happy people who enjoy laughter. On the other hand, if I told you I like dark colors, you might assume I'm a serious professional who does not like to laugh.

3. **Intimate conversation** develops when we share our deep feelings with another. There is an increased risk of being hurt or abandoned because the information is more personal. I take a risk, for example with you as a reader, in telling you that I grew up on a farm. You could make the assumption that my parents grew vegetables and raised cattle. You might not expect that I am a licensed therapist with several college degrees and educational awards to my credit.

4. **Peak communication** occurs when we talk about our feelings about our mutual relationship. A man becomes vulnerable and takes a great risk when he tells a woman he loves her. He gives her the power to shatter his heart or create a new and deeper relationship.

Again, Christ is our example. He poured a great deal of himself and his time into teaching, correcting, and loving his disciples. He daily risked rejection of himself and his teachings but did not shy away from relationships because of it.

How Do You Meet Strangers?

During my early teen years, I was extremely awkward and shy. My youth leader wanted all of us to meet new people who'd come to our group, so he gave us an assignment. We had to make a list of questions we could use to get to know any person. I've since used this tool with my patients to help them engage new people in conversation. Some of our questions included:

1. What is your favorite food?
2. What is your favorite book or movie?
3. What is the farthest you have traveled away from your home?
4. Which is your favorite sports team?
5. What television character do you like most?
6. What did you like most about your parents?
7. What was the funniest thing you ever did?
8. What was your favorite subject in school?
9. What was your favorite vacation?

I find that questions are a communications door that opens and unlocks the entrance to relationships. Throughout the Gospels, Jesus masterfully used questions to form relationships. A good example of his skill is the story of the woman at the well.

Jesus had been traveling a long distance and stopped at a well, where he met a woman. He was thirsty and he asked her to meet his need. "Would you give me a drink of water?" She chose to address his need by giving him what he asked for. In return, he offered her living water, "gushing fountains of endless life." Then he told her to call her husband. Since she had been divorced several times and had apparently not married her current partner, she had to confess her sin and folly. Her admission freed her from her bondage of secrecy. She left her jar at the well, and ran to tell the people in the surrounding countryside of her new salvation (see John 4, *The Message*).

How Do You Get Beneath the Surface?

Jesus used questions to get beneath the surface to the woman's pain. The questions in the list above will help you start a conversation, but they don't move beyond surface issues. So how can you move beyond the mundane in your relationships? "Monster carrots" provide a clue.

In the Seattle area, there is a community where farmers grow a special variety of carrots. "Monster carrots," as they're called, grow to two to three pounds each by fall. I remember the first time my mother saw them, she refused to purchase them thinking they'd be tough and bitter. One day she finally bought some, and they were the most sweet and tender carrots we'd ever eaten. The next fall, we made a special trip to the farm and purchased sacks of these carrots to freeze for soups, stews, and special vegetable dishes. It was their size and looks that dissuaded us from initially tasting these delicacies.

I later realized that communication is like one of those carrots. From the surface, all you see is a light green stalk. But if you pull on that stalk, you will find a big carrot underneath. You have to be willing to dig below the surface to find the tasty vegetable that is one of my favorites.

Sometimes we are intimidated by someone's size, education, social or economic status. These surface characteristics hinder us from tasting goodness that comes from legitimate relationship. I urge you not to let potentially great relationships remain undiscovered because of fear and intimidation.

Where Do I Go to Find Relationships?

Those who've been deeply hurt and isolated for a prolonged time need to be patient with themselves. It will take time and effort to learn to trust again. You might start by taking a class or learning a new hobby. Check your local newspaper's weekend section for interesting things to do in your area. Anxiety often blinds us to the opportunities around us, so don't be afraid to try new things.

These new activities will help you overcome an anxiety disorder by distracting you from your worry and helping you to connect with people. Remember the objective in these activities is to do them *with* people in hopes of building a trusting relationship with individuals. Doing these activities alone will not help you form relationships!

How Have Relationships Affected Your Life?

Undoubtedly relationships have created both great sorrow and great joy in your life. If you've been hurt, you may feel hesitant about opening your heart again. When my own life caved in, God used significant relationships to start the process of healing my broken heart and restoring my life.

When I was fourteen, my treasured life in the country ended abruptly when Father decided to build a new house for Mother in celebration of their upcoming twenty-fifth wedding anniversary. She often told him she didn't need the house to be happy. It was more important to her to have a healthy and happy family. But Father loved Mother and he wanted to give her the house of her dreams. We worked hard in the family business, preparing for the time when Mother's dream house would be built.

When I was in junior high school, construction on the house began. I remember coming home from school each day and seeing the progress of the foundation, walls, siding, and finally paint. The building of the house was the subject of much conversation in our little farming community. My father took special care in custom-designing many unique features especially for Mother.

One of the last projects to be completed was the watering system that was fed by our well. The contractor had difficulty connecting the well, and asked Father and some of his workmen to help him. Father crawled down into the deep trench. One of the men asked him a question, and he looked up to answer. Suddenly, my father literally saw red. He was rushed to the emergency room where it was discovered that a piece of scar tissue from his heart had come loose—a complication from a childhood bout with rheumatic fever—and lodged behind his eye. Blood thinners were used in an attempt to save his sight in that eye. Unbeknownst to the doctors, the blood thinners accelerated another physical problem that had not yet been diagnosed.

While he was in the hospital, Father told the doctors he was having problems eating. Tests revealed something wrong with his stomach. Fear overtook our family as we immediately recalled that his mother had died of stomach cancer and his younger brother had died of a brain tumor.

Days passed with no new information. Each specialist Father saw ordered another test. Finally, he was diagnosed with terminal stomach cancer. Doctors operated the next day, hoping to save his life.

I remember the day of the operation. My parents gave me the option of going to school or to the hospital. I went to school that day and pretended nothing was wrong. I was in gym class when over the loud speaker, the principal said, "Will Carol Christensen please come to the office? Her mother is here to pick her up."

My heart sank when I heard these words; I knew something had gone wrong with the surgery. I quickly changed my clothes, darted to the office where I found my mother crying.

"Regardless of the outcome of your father's operation," Mother told me, "we determined to tell you the truth. The surgeon cut your father open," she blurted, "took one look at his stomach, and sewed him back up."

Mother hesitated, attempting to contain her emotions before she concluded. "Your father is dying, and the doctors can't do any more for him. They think it's best for us to be there with him when they tell him his cancer is terminal."

"How long does he have?" I asked Mother.

She looked desperately into my eyes and continued. "About two years. It will take him some time to recover from the operation, but the doctors say we can still go on the trip we were planning to take this spring. We'll still move into the house and celebrate our twenty-fifth wedding anniversary, and we'll have plenty of time to do whatever we need to before he dies."

"But Mother," I said, "I don't understand. Why is God doing this to us?"

"We'll talk about that later. Right now we have to get your brother from his grade school and get to the hospital before your father wakes up. The doctors say he will need our love and support to get through this."

We did get to the hospital before Father woke. I remember feeling intimidated in his room when a swarm of men in white coats entered. Mother later explained that Father was in a teaching hospital, and these men were interns. Father's case was difficult, and his only hope was to have doctors who had the most advanced knowledge of medicine.

The doctors told my father of his prognosis, and I will never forget the look on their faces as he responded to their report. With boldness and calm assurance, he told these men that he did not fear death because he knew he was going home to be with his Lord and Savior, Jesus Christ. Looking back, I can see God's hand in exposing a group of young doctors, who would go on to impact many others, to the Gospel.

Not only did his testimony affect their lives, but mine as well. My father's confident words left an indelible impression on my young heart and caused me to question my own faith. *If I were dying in that bed, would I be that assured of my eternal destination? Is my faith that strong?*

Father and Mother later met privately with the doctors. They decided that Father would come home to live in our new house before he died. Though Father's friends were devastated when they heard the news, they helped us quickly move our belongings into our new dream house.

My parents' new bedroom was transformed into a makeshift hospital room, and to my dismay, it seemed that everyone we knew stopped by to pay their last respects.

Shortly after he came home, Father's condition dramatically and unexpectedly worsened. We soon had to face certain excruciating realities: We would not be taking our much-anticipated trip abroad; my father would not see me graduate from high school or college; he would not give me away at my wedding or see his grandchildren.

As a family, we gained comfort and strength by reading the Bible, praying, and sharing together. Our pastor came several times a week to minister to our family, but our swelling emotions were becoming more and more difficult to contain.

I was concerned about Mother and tried to lighten her load by helping her care for my father. His pain was so great that he needed strong pain medicine every four hours. I hated helping Mother give him the Demerol shots and then listening as he verbally relived his life.

In addition to the shots, Father still couldn't eat. He required round-the-clock intravenous feedings to sustain his life. I remember watching helplessly as I saw the body of a strong man shrink into a fragile skeleton.

At that time, computers did not monitor medical equipment; Mother and I had to watch it all with our own eyes, bearing the responsibility for my father's survival. We soon developed a plan—Mother would watch the intravenous feeding equipment for two hours while I tried to sleep, and then we would switch.

I remember going to my room one night and turning up the volume on the television so Mother would not hear me as I cried. "God, take him home," I prayed, "I can't bear to watch him suffer any more."

God did answer my prayer shortly thereafter. One day a friend drove me to the pharmacy to get morphine for my father. I knew morphine was a last resort, so I was afraid that Father was near death.

By the time we came home, he was being loaded into the ambulance to go to the hospital. He died that night of heart failure. Father lived a total of three-and-a-half weeks in our new home before he died.

"Why did God have to let such a good man die?" people asked me at his funeral. "Your father was such a good man," they said to me. "You were really lucky to have such a wonderful man for a father."

The first spring without Father was difficult. That year several of Father's friends helped Mother sell the spring crops. My parents were technically considered farmers, though they didn't raise cows or chickens, but flowers. That spring, we raised tulips that were planted in the fall, geraniums, fuchsia baskets and a whole host of other plants. In the summer, Mother sold the business, the property, and the dream house that had been built especially for her.

We moved to the city, where I started my sophomore year in high school. It was quite a transition from farm to city life. I no longer had work with perishable flowers after school. I no longer had 4-H club projects to complete, a garden to plant, or a pig to care for. Suddenly I was thrust into a world of after-school clubs, snow skiing, and other leisure activities. I didn't know how to cope with all the free time and materialism I was faced with day after day. Life in the city was such a contrast to the farm and the many hours of work during the spring seasons when most of the flowers were sold.

I began to hang around a group of teens that didn't understand my pain. They lived a lifestyle that was much different from mine. Although I didn't drink and party like they did, I was exposed to a different value system. I had been raised in the church, and I could see that their activities were not good. Still, I felt so empty on the inside, and I was so angry at God, that I was strongly tempted to follow after this crowd. In my heart, though, I knew getting drunk was not the answer.

There was another group of students on my campus who were involved in a Christian group. Some of my friends from church attended their activities, and I remember a senior boy who was the group's leader. He carried the biggest black leather Bible I'd ever seen. He often read it before class, and during the first semester, he attempted to corner me between classes. I was angry with God, and I didn't want to hear it.

One day I saw him coming and ducked into the girl's restroom before he could get to me. He was persistent, though, and I eventually gave in and talked to him. I questioned my faith, and he had answers. He invited me to a Bible study at his home, but I refused for a long time. Inside my heart, I grew cold and empty and withdrawn. Finally, one afternoon I decided I'd go to his study. I knew I needed help, but my pride wouldn't allow me to acknowledge it to anybody.

I had a really good time at the study and attended many other Christian events. I eventually met a woman I will call Susan who volunteered with my group. She began to spend time with me and we developed a special relationship. I didn't have my driver's license, so she picked me up in her old white car for our evening group meetings. All of the kids in our group thought she was really cool, so I felt privileged to have her as my special adult friend.

When Susan brought me home after meetings, she lovingly listened to me talk about my pain, often until the early hours of the morning. She was a "safe person" for me. Although she wasn't a professional counselor, the Lord used her to begin to heal and mend the broken places in my life. Susan was God's gift to me to help me through that period in my life. I was blessed to have an older woman help me. When I later became a youth leader, my desire was to help others the way Susan had helped me.

As I look back on my life, I am thankful for the many rich relationships God brought during the tough times. When I took the initiative to ask for help, God brought a caring, Christian person to come alongside me during times of great difficulty. My mind drifts to our associate pastor who helped me when my mother was dying; my girlfriend who encouraged me to start working in a psychiatric hospital; my brother, who encouraged me to return to school for my master's degree when I was older than many other college students; another girlfriend who encouraged me to write the proposal for this book even though I was very ill; my clinical supervisor, who encouraged me to take my state boards for licensure as a therapist. All of these people lovingly supported me when I didn't think I could continue on. God used each of these individuals to help me during a time of crisis.

In the book of Ecclesiastes, the Bible reminds us, "With a friend you can face the worst. Can you round up a third? A three-stranded rope isn't easily broken" (Ecclesiastes 4:11, *The Message*). As in the illustration of the rope, we become stronger when we have the support of a couple of friends. Each of us needs the love and support of others who will encourage us to continue on the path that God has set before us.

As you struggle with anxiety, whom can you seek out for support and comfort? Who will encourage you when you want to give up but know you need to continue on? I encourage you to avoid isolation and open your heart to relationship. You will find, as I have countless times, God will use them to help you when you don't think you can carry on. "Therefore encourage one another and build each other up ..." (1 Thessalonians 5:11a).

Power Tools

Power Padlock: I'm not getting any better at managing my anxiety.

Power Principle: God is committed to helping me grow and develop as a person.

Power Passage: "Being confident of this, that he who began a good work in you will perfect it until the day of Christ Jesus" (Philippians 1:6).

Power Question: What steps can I take today that will highlight I trust him to bring about long-term healing in my life?

Power Padlock: I've learned how to reduce my anxiety and I don't have to do anything more.

Power Principle: The managing of my anxiety will be a life-long journey.

Power Passage: "Not that I have already obtained all this, or have already been made perfect, but I press on to take hold of that for which Christ Jesus took hold of me" (Philippians 3:12).

Power Question: Who will hold me accountable to continue my deep breathing and other relaxation techniques?

Power Padlock: I don't want to bother anyone to help me manage my anxiety.

Power Principle: Even the apostle Paul needed friends to support and encourage him.

Power Passage: "Epaphras, my fellow prisoner in Christ Jesus, send you greetings. And so do Mark, Aristarchus, Demas,and Luke, my fellow workers" (Philemon 23–24).

Power Question: Who can I tell about my anxiety today that can provide love and support for the management of my anxieties?

Power Padlock: My needs for support and encouragement are not important.

Power Principle: We are all part of the body of Christ and can reach out to others for our needs.

Power Passage: "Now you are the body of Christ, and each one of you is a part of it" (1 Corinthians 12:27).

Power Question: This week, how will I let someone love me?

Doctor's or psychiatrist's evaluation for medications

Instructions for a crisis plan

Self-control of your body

Church or community groups for support

Halting any notion of being a lone ranger

Activities to expand relationships

Resuming your regular schedule

Guidance from others

Evaluation for other services

Preparing for future anxiety

Leaving time for practicing relaxation techniques

Assuming adult responsibility for learning to relax your body

Naming your accountability sources

12 Your Discharge Plan:
Transitioning to Self-Management

"I'm tired of trying to manage my panic. Last night I almost swallowed a bottle of pills," Paula confessed to the group. "I live in constant fear of having another attack in public! I'm sick of doing deep breathing and those other relaxation exercises. I want to escape—I can't take it anymore—and I want to die!"

The group members' eyes widened and they were speechless. Their concern for Paula was evident, and Paula realized that she could be overreacting. Calming a bit, Paula continued to voice her frustration.

"My anxiety is getting worse," Paula confessed. "I've been coming to group for over a year now, but I'm having panic attacks more frequently again. I'm regressing—I'm afraid to leave my house—I'm not ready for discharge!"

Debbie looked at Paula. "Do you remember a few weeks ago when I told the group that when people prepare for discharge, anxiety can sometimes increase?"

"No, I forgot all about it," Paula admitted. "Is this what you meant?"

"Yes. I was preparing you and the rest of the group for leaving treatment. It's normal to experience increased anxiety at discharge when the group disbands and there is a loss of support from others. Many of the members grow close to one another through the group experience, so by the time the group terminates, they feel as if they're losing significant relationships. I encourage you to exchange telephone numbers and e-mail addresses so you can keep in touch with each other."

"Can you keep yourself safe, and do you agree not to harm yourself?" Debbie asked Paula.

"Yes," she answered, "I can."

"If at any time you think you're suicidal," Debbie asked Paula, "will you promise to call a friend, 9-1-1, or page me before you hurt yourself? Will you go to an emergency room for help?"

"Yes," Paula said in agreement.

Debbie paused to look at the other group members before she returned to Paula. "Let's do some reality testing. Remember, with anxiety, we exaggerate our fears. You're a bright woman, Paula, and I know you'll do just fine. You'll need to continue to manage your anxiety and open yourself up to new relationships to get well."

"But I don't have any friends," Paula protested to Debbie. "I'm retired, and I don't see people at work anymore. I've never taken much time to develop relationships outside this group."

"Perhaps you're going to take adult responsibility to make some new friends," Debbie encouraged.

"I don't know where to look for friends," Paula continued in a helpless victim tone.

"A good place to start is with your church," Debbie explained. "In most churches, there are a variety of activities for people of all ages. There are women's and men's Bible study groups, prayer meetings, choir and other musical activities, and many service opportunities for youth and senior groups. There are also many support groups springing up in various churches."

"I don't feel like I'm an elderly person *yet*," Paula said bristling.

"Of course not," Debbie decided to use Paula's irritation to teach her more about anxiety. "What are you experiencing now? Has your anxiety gone away?"

"Well, yes," Paula replied in surprise.

Debbie continued encouragingly, "As a human being, it is impossible to be anxious and angry at the same time. You need to get your feelings out in the open and start sharing them with others. It's good for you to share what you are feeling with us. You've got a whole lot of life in you yet to live. However, you can choose to live it like a hermit in a dark, lonely cave, or you can step out and bask in the warmth of loving relationships."

"I've been thinking about taking a cooking class at the community college. Could that help me?"

"Absolutely," Debbie replied. "The best situations are those that encourage you to share your joys and sorrows—and even everyday life—with others. You could take a photography, watercolor, computer, or woodworking class—*anything* that helps you get out and develop relationships. You'll need them to manage your anxiety away from group."

Debbie addressed the whole group: "You're more likely to have problems managing your anxiety during major life crisis points, such as retirement, marriage, birth of a child, illness, and so forth. Because you have an anxiety disorder, using the tools we've talked about to gain self-control over your body will be critical during times of stress."

"What do you mean 'self-control'?" Jan interrupted Debbie. "I think of control in terms of not overeating, avoiding sexual sin, not overindulging in alcohol, or not using illegal drugs."

Debbie responded further, "Self-control isn't just about avoiding sin or temptation. The person with an anxiety disorder needs to focus on learning to control her body's response to her anxiety."

"This is the last week of the session," Jan reminded Debbie. "Why haven't you mentioned this before now?"

"I have," Debbie told Jan, "I think your anxiety is confusing and disorganizing your memory. We have talked about methods such as 'anxiety management,' 'control,' 'stewardship,' 'adult responsibility,' and many other labels to describe what you've been learning. All these terms describe the kind of self-control you will need to successfully manage your anxiety in the future."

As Debbie prepared to discharge the patients from group she added, "Remember that managing your anxiety is a process. It will take time to apply the information we've discussed here. You are more knowledgeable and better prepared to manage your anxiety, but you will need to practice and strengthen your anxiety management skills. She paused before she added: "I believe you are very capable of doing that."

Debbie also praised each member for the progress they'd made. Together they stood and thanked God for the new skills they'd learned, for the new relationships they'd formed, and for the new hope they'd gained for the future. As tears filled their eyes, they moved closer together and embraced each other in a last group hug. Their discharge was complete.

How Does One Terminate Therapy?

Therapy has a beginning, a middle, and an end. The end is called discharge. It is an essential part of the process of getting better and follows involvement in group or individual therapy. A slow and gradual transition often makes it easier, and a good therapist will carefully move a patient through steadily increasing steps of responsibility toward the management and stewardship of his or her life before discharge.

It is important to understand that there are a number of different levels in the therapeutic process. Some patients start in an intense inpatient psychiatric facility. In cases where patients have attempted to take their own lives or otherwise significantly harm themselves, staff members provide basic support functions needed to sustain life. These can include help with eating, sleeping, and basic grooming. As the person's condition improves, the responsibility for these basic functions is slowly transferred back to the patient.

Once they are discharged from an inpatient psychiatric facility, it is becoming increasingly popular for patients to continue therapy in a day treatment or intense outpatient program where they are involved in treatment all day, but go home at night. These programs often pack several months of therapy into a few short weeks and have a high rate of success.

With the skyrocketing costs of hospitalization, today's average hospital stay for inpatient mental health services is only 3–5 days—not nearly enough time to educate and equip a patient for successful management of anxiety disorder. A day program provides the encouragement to learn skills and develop new behaviors within the context of a structured environment without the high cost of hospitalization. These programs help to fill the gaps between inpatient and outpatient counseling.

A combination of individual, family, or group counseling is next. The patient might begin by seeing a therapist once a week, biweekly, and then monthly in preparation for discharge into a group setting. Groups are often used to further work on relational issues that might not be addressed in an individual session.

For some people, group therapy is the quickest intervention because of the intensity and focus on relational issues. In group, individuals work on relational issues with their therapist and with other group members. For example, a man who hates women finds himself in a group full of women. In group he will have to work on interacting with female members in an appropriate way.

Following these professional levels of intervention, the patient is discharged to a 12-step support group, pastor or lay counselor, or other forms of church or community support. These could include support groups, church activities, or other non-clinical environments where patients can receive the love and community support needed to transition into "normal" life.

Usually a discharge plan is developed to encourage long-term recovery and growth. It provides a "safety net" as one ventures to establish a new life away from therapy.

How Long Will the Process of Discharge Take?

From the day a patient enters any form of treatment, the therapist is working on a plan to help the person discharge. I often joke with my patients that this is one job where my primary task is to work myself *out* of work! It is my hope as a therapist that my patients will manage their anxiety on their own, but I assure them that I will be there to provide emotional support and encouragement if the journey becomes too difficult.

People with anxiety disorders need to realize that they are capable of managing their anxiety. By practicing the deep breathing, relaxation techniques, thought stopping, and meditation, coupled with a good discharge plan, they can resume a healthy, productive life. For the good of the patient, therapists do not coddle or enable people with anxiety disorder. The challenge of therapy is to help increase the patient's autonomy, responsibility, and self-control. They need to learn to stop playing the role of a helpless child and start taking adult responsibility for their lives.

What Can I Expect from Others after I Discharge from Therapy?

People respond differently to mental illness than they do to physical illness or injury. For example, if you go to a hospital and have back surgery, your surgeon will want you up on your feet as soon as possible. However, you will not immediately resume your normal activities completely. A transition is still needed.

When you discharge from the hospital, you will have a brace on your back. At home, you will ease back into your activities. You would go to your doctor on a weekly, and then a monthly basis. Enjoy any special attention you receive from family or friends, because when your short transition period is complete, you will return to work and assume your normal schedule.

Unlike a physical operation, however, an anxiety disorder isn't readily apparent; people don't see the invisible bandages on your heart. They don't understand that you are enduring a transition and need love and support to resume your life. They may not even acknowledge that you've been in treatment. And you may prefer not to tell others you have been in treatment. As much as you're able, don't let the reactions of others bother you. Discuss potential reactions with your therapist before your discharge and get help in anticipating how others may respond.

What Ingredients Are Involved in the Discharge Plan?

Not too long ago, a friend of mine rented a car to drive us from the Tampa airport to a conference in Florida. I had not been in that state since college, and I didn't have a good sense of exactly where we were going. Once we were settled in the car, we pulled out a map and followed the step-by-step directions so we would be certain to get to the conference on time. A discharge plan is simply a map that lays out your road toward recovery.

When you invited Jesus Christ to come into your life, you started on a new journey. Now you are walking the road to healing and redemption, which will not be complete until you go home to be with him. In the meantime, healing is a process that continues as long as we live here on earth. In Philippians 1:6, the Bible reminds us that we can be confident "that he who began a good work in you will carry it on to completion until the day of Jesus Christ."

When I completed my bachelor's degree, I had the opportunity to travel to the Middle East. One morning I watched the sun rise over the Sea of Galilee in Israel. It was inspiring to see the giant lake that I'd read about so often in the Gospels and realize it hadn't changed much since Jesus had walked its shores. Early each morning, the local fishermen still cast their nets from boats much like those used by Peter, James, and John. With those nets, the fishermen provide for their families and their futures.

I learned that when the nets were broken, the fishermen would bring them on shore to "restore" them. Mending the fishing net was not just a matter of patching a whole or repairing a tear. The fishermen's goal was to mend the net so it is even stronger than before the damage.

In the New Testament, the Bible uses the word "restore" in conjunction with our lives. First Peter 5:10 says, "And the God of all grace, who called you to his eternal glory in Christ, after you have suffered a little while, will himself restore you and make you strong, firm and steadfast." The idea is that Christ will mend or "restore" our lives so we are stronger than we were before. In God's plan, the pain, distress, fears, and confusion that are underneath an anxiety disorder are addressed so that we can live with new strength and purpose.

With this background, think of a discharge plan as a way of mending your net. A discharge plan can provide the ingredients needed for continued growth or restoration. Your therapist may just discuss it with you—like someone giving you directions. Or, it may be in written form, more like a map. Either way, it is a short plan that is generally used to evaluate your progress, determine your next steps, and may include instructions or recommendations for the following:

Medication. If medications are involved, discharge involves a continued monitoring by a licensed provider for medications. In some cases, medications can be slowly tapered. In other cases, such as moderate to severe Panic and OCD, medications may continue for some time. Don't suddenly stop taking medication without discussing your plan with your medical doctor or psychiatrist.

Deferred matters. During treatment, it may be necessary to postpone or defer addressing underlying or subordinate issues. If there are issues that have been deferred during treatment, they are generally addressed at discharge. These could include family counseling, physical problems, and some addiction issues. Referrals to other agencies or specialists are considered at this point.

12-step and church-sponsored groups. Recommendations to 12-step support groups in churches or communities are often included. They are easy to get to and there are usually a number of groups in any community focusing on substance abuse, gambling, eating disorders, codependency, grief, etc. The primary difference between 12-step groups and therapy groups or other forms of treatment is that 12-step groups are not usually led by a trained professional.

Activities. Activities that get you involved with others are highly encouraged. Examples include church Bible studies, women's and men's groups, youth groups, and so on. Many other activities are available outside the church, including fitness classes, college courses, and community education.

Crisis plan. A plan is created for what the patient can do if the symptoms return or if he feels suicidal. He can go to the ER, call 9-1-1, contact a therapist, or call a friend.

Reminders of success. The plan reviews progress and helps to remind the patient of successes. Just as the Israelites built altars and piles of stones to remember God's work in the wilderness, so we too need to build reminders that celebrate the changes in our behavior. We need to stop and thank God for what he has enabled us to accomplish on our journey. And we need those markers to point to when success seems elusive.

Some people find it helpful to write out the Scriptures of promise, healing, and restoration, such as the ones we've discussed in this book. Writing God's loving truth in your own hand may help you to remember his promises and see just how personally they apply to you.

Why Are Transitions Difficult?

As a growth step, transitions are difficult even when we know they are for our good. Yet you have already lived through many transitions successfully. Every toddler transitions from crawling to walking—a process that can be frustrating and painful. The first day of school, puberty, graduation, marriage—all are milestones of life that require a change in us—a transition from what was to what is to what will be. Transitions are difficult because change is difficult. But where there is the ability and willingness to change, there is also hope.

During my senior year in high school, I experienced the transition from farm life to city life following the death of my father. As is often true, God sometimes allows circumstances in our lives that change us. It is not always clear why he has allowed these transitions. But sometimes he gives us a glimpse of how he is working everything together for our good. A particularly traumatic situation made it very clear to me how the difficult transition to the city was part of God's plan for me.

As a graduating senior, I was required to take a "family living" class. One

Friday morning we had a guest speaker who talked about suicide. She said that if we knew someone who was suicidal, we should contact someone immediately by calling 9-1-1 or alerting other mental health professionals or health care providers. We need to love with limits, she reminded us. We would need to give that person hope but we would also need to set appropriate boundaries.

That night my friends and I planned to meet at the beach for a walk at sunset. We loved to build a campfire there (it was legal then!), roast marshmallows, and sing and pray together. But when I got there, only one other girl was there. Tammy hung out with our Christian group occasionally, but a didn't know her well. Not wanting to miss the sunset, she and I decided not to wait for the others. I never expected what would happen as we left our cars and started our walk along the peaceful beach.

The waters of Puget Sound lapped against the shore as the setting sun shot rays of vibrant pink, purple, and lavender across the sky. God and I had reached an understanding, and I was at peace with him and my life in the city that day. Suddenly my peace was shattered by Tammy's screaming. "My father doesn't love me! My mother nags me constantly! I hate my sister with her perfect 4.0, and my little brother is driving me crazy! Life isn't worth living!" With that final proclamation, Tammy pulled a knife from her pocket. *This must be a joke!* I thought as I tried to tease Tammy about the knife. But the look of deep pain in her eyes as she glared at me soon convinced me otherwise. Over the pounding of my heart, questions flew through my mind. *But why?* I wondered frantically. *This doesn't make sense!* My friend seemed to have everything—she was part of a prominent family in our community, she had her own sports car, credit cards with no limits—and she was beautiful besides. *What more could you want?* I wanted to ask her. She had everything I thought a girl could want—money, beauty, and brains. *Why would she want to throw it all away?*

In the seconds it took for these thoughts to flash through my mind, Tammy lunged toward me placing the blade of the knife to my throat. "You're going to die first, and then I'm going to kill myself!"

"I hate you!" Tammy screamed. "All of you Christians think you're so perfect. You don't know what it's like to live in a home where your father gets drunk and beats you just because you're there."

I could hardly breathe, yet I scrambled for words. "You're right!" I blurted. "There was never anything like that in my home. I had my share of problems when my father died, but I never had to deal with anything like that."

The words of the speaker from family living class suddenly came back to me: *You've got to give the suicidal person hope.* I prayed, *Dear Lord, what hope can I give to Tammy?*

Even as I prayed, Tammy began to cry. Slowly she dropped the knife and fell to her knees. There in the sand, I shared the hope of the Gospel with the girl who had just threatened to kill me.

Remembering I needed to love with limits, I took Tammy to meet with Susan, a youth worker I trusted. Together, Susan and I helped Tammy recommit her life to Christ and find a structured mental health treatment program that would help her address the painful issues in her life. This was the beginning of an 8-year healing process to help Tammy face her problems.

It was then that I also began to realize my need to learn about boundaries and limits. Watching Tammy, I knew I had to start facing my own issues. If I wanted to help other people grow, I had to begin learning about my own pain and injuries. Even though Tammy rededicated her life to Christ that night, her struggles didn't end there; she had many other mountains yet to climb. She did start to grow in her faith, but I saw some things that concerned me.

One night I was home alone watching TV. The main character in the program was an alcoholic who went to his first Alcoholics Anonymous meeting. At the end of the show, a phone number for AA was given. I called and had information sent to me about alcoholism. Tammy showed many of the symptoms the pamphlet described, so I confronted her. She denied that her drinking was out of control, but later she told me how she hid alcohol in her locker. She bragged that she put it into her coffee and drank it in front of our teachers. Tammy agreed that she had a problem, but she was afraid to go alone to her first meeting, so we attended AA together. Later, I was honored when she gave me her seven-year sobriety pin as a token of her appreciation for my support. Her recovery included many of the other issues I now deal with every day in my counseling practice.

Looking back to those years, I can see that the most difficult part of the transition from the farm to the city was the depths of the need I encountered. My friends and acquaintances saw my home and family as a haven of stability and strength. These students called me at all hours, looking for help. At one point, my family had to establish boundaries to help me get enough sleep.

One day, a few years after my beach encounter with Tammy, my mother and I were talking. "You know one of the reasons God took your father home, don't you?"

"Well," I said, "I think so, but why do you think he did?"

"I think He wanted to prepare you for a life of helping others," Mother told me. "When we moved to the city, your eyes were opened to the world. I don't think you would have seen in the country what you've seen here. You've seen kids who've had every material possession and are still unhappy. I think you've learned an important lesson about life values and priorities in terms of your spiritual life.

"Remember Pastor's sermon this morning?" Mother continued. "He told us about a wealthy son who looked at the world and saw it was 'vanity.' Nothing he saw made sense. He saw that power, wealth, beauty, and prestige were not going to fill the void in his heart. He came to the conclusion that the only important thing was to remember your Creator in the days of your youth.

"As I look at you," Mother continued, "I think of your grandmother Christensen. I remember a day when I felt as if my world had fallen apart. A storm had destroyed all our crops in the greenhouse. We thought we'd lost everything in our business.

"Your grandmother gave me a Bible, and I opened it and read Isaiah 40:8, which says, 'The grass withers and the flowers fall, but the word of our God stands forever.' That was when I knew that God really cared about me and my circumstances."

Mother was not raised in the church, but she told me that she prayed and asked Christ into her heart that day. He was the One who helped her through all of the fears she endured losing my father, raising two children as a single parent, and starting a new life in the city.

She got choked up before she could continue. "I think your grandmother's mantle has passed to you. Just like Elijah passed on his ministry to Elisha, you're the one in our family to carry on the ministry."

Suddenly, my whole world made sense. Although I'd only just embarked on the journey of my own recovery and healing, I sensed it was a process that would include many peaks and valleys before my path would lead me home to the Father. As I began to prepare for this ministry, I had to learn about providing truth, reality, and responsibility. During the early days, it was hard for me to realize that loving someone meant I cared enough to establish limits on their behavior.

Today, I realize I'm still in process—and so are you. Perhaps you are considering for the first time that you or someone you love may have an anxiety disorder. Or, maybe you've already been in therapy for a very long time. Wherever you are in your journey, remember that every step you take toward healing is a victory to be celebrated. Power over panic or any anxiety disorder will come as you learn to control your body, to take adult responsibility for your life, and to ask for help when you need it.

Never give up hope! In my practice I've seen countless people just like Mike, Paula, Sarah, Steve, Christina, and Jan—people who thought their lives were a hopeless mess. I've watched them choose to take active responsibility for their future, learn to manage their anxiety, and gain control over the effects of anxiety in their lives.

Whatever your circumstances, you can learn to manage your disorder. You can learn new boundaries and open yourself to love again. The battle for power over panic won't be won in a single skirmish, however. Choose today to keep fighting, to keep moving forward. Take Christ with you into the battle and you will never fight alone. With his help, there is power over panic and answers for anxiety. Others have done it—so can you!

Notes

Chapter 1: What Is Anxiety?

1. Satcher, David, M.D., Ph.D., Surgeon General, (1999). Mental Health: A Report from the Surgeon General: Chapter 4. 10/09/02. Washington, D.C.: U.S. Government Printing Office, Retrieved from the Worldwide Web: http://surgeongenral.gov/library/mentalhealth/chapter4/sec2.html
2. Discovery Health Features, 02/01/02, *Fires of the Mind: Generalized Anxiety Disorder.* 10/10/02. Retrieved from the Worldwide Web: http://health.discovey.com/convergence/fires/anxiety7.html
3. University of Phoenix, MSN Learning & Research Plus, n.d. *Anxiety: Generalized Anxiety Disorder,* 10/10/02. Retrieved from the Worldwide Web: http://encarta.msn.com/encnet/refpages/RefArticle.aspx?refid+761562471&para=7
4. Mental Help Net, Staff, n.d. *Introduction: Anxiety Disorders.* 10/12/02. Retrieved from the Worldwide Web: http://mentalhelp.net/poc/center_index.php?id=1
5. Satcher, David, M.D., Ph.D., Surgeon General, (1999) *Mental Health: A Report from the Surgeon General:* Chapter 4. 10/09/02. Washington, D.C.: U.S. Government Printing Office, Retrieved from the Worldwide Web: http://surgeongenral.gov/library/mentalhealth/chapter4/sec2.html
6. Mental Help Net, Staff, n.d. *Introduction: Anxiety Disorders.* 10/12/02. Retrieved from the Worldwide Web: http://mentalhelp.net/poc/center_index.php?id=1
7. ibid.
8. ibid.

Chapter 2: Generalized Anxiety Disorder

1. Reprinted with permission from the *Diagnostic and Statistical Manual of Mental Disorders,* Fourth Edition, Text Revision. Copyright 2000, American Psychiatric Association.
2. National Institute of Mental Health. (1999). *Facts About Generalized Anxiety Disorder,* (NIMH Publication No. OM-99 4153 revised,) Bethesda, MD.
3. DuPont, Dr. Robert, Dr. Caroline DuPont, & Elizabeth DuPont, Spencer, LCSW-C, *Generalized Anxiety Disorder: A Clinicians Guide to "the Worry Disease."* In Directions in Clinical & Counseling Psychology, Frederick Flach, MD, (Editor-In-Chief), Volume 9, Lesson 12, p. 147. New York, NY: Hatherleigh Company, Ltd., 147.
4. ibid., 146.
5. Gliatto, Michael F. 10/01/00, *Generalized Anxiety Disorder.* Retrieved from the Worldwide Web: http://www.findarticles.com/cf_dls/m3225/7_62/65864095/p1/article.jhtml.

6. DuPont, Dr. Robert, Dr. Caroline DuPont, & Elizabeth DuPont, Spencer, LCSW-C, *Generalized Anxiety Disorder: A Clinicians Guide to "the Worry Disease."* In Directions in Clinical & Counseling Psychology, Frederick Flach, MD, (Editor-In-Chief), Volume 9, Lesson 12, p. 146. New York, NY: Hatherleigh Company, Ltd.

7. ibid., 147.

8. ibid., 147.

9. ibid., 146.

10. ibid., 146.

11. Hamilton, Karen, 06/28/99. Anxiety/Panic Disorder: *The High Anxiety Personality*, Retrieved from the Worldwide Web: http://www.suite101.com/article.cfm/panic_disorder/21756.

Chapter 3: Social Phobia

1. Reprinted with permission from the *Diagnostic and Statistical Manual of Mental Disorders,* Fourth Edition, Text Revision. Copyright 2000, American Psychiatric Association.

2. Richards, Thomas A., Ph.D., n.d. Social Anxiety Network: *What is Social Anxiety/Social Phobia?* 10/12/02. Retrieved from the Worldwide Web: http://www.anxietynetwork.com/spwhat.html.

3. The Ohio State University, Anxiety and Stress Disorders Clinic, n.d. *Social Phobia,* 10/09/02. Retrieved from the Worldwide Web: http://anxiety.psy.ohio-state/SocialPhobia.htm.

4. Richards, Thomas A., Ph.D., n.d. Social Anxiety Network: *Fact Sheet,* 10/14/02 Retrieved on the Worldwide Web: http://www.socialphobia.org/fact.html.

5. Richards, Thomas A., Ph.D., n.d. Social Anxiety Network: *What is Social Anxiety/Social Phobia?* 10/12/02. Retrieved from the Worldwide Web: http://www.anxietynetwork.com/spwhat.html.

6. The Ohio State University, Anxiety and Stress Disorders Clinic, n.d. *Social Phobia,* 10/09/02. Retrieved from the Worldwide Web: http://anxiety.psy.ohio-state/SocialPhobia.htm.

7. Mental Help Net, Staff, n.d. *Introduction: Anxiety Disorders.* 10/12/02. Retrieved from the Worldwide Web: http://mentalhelp.net/poc/center_index.php?id=1.

8. Open-mind, (11/15/99) *Social Anxiety Disorder: A Common, Underrecognized Mental Disorder.* (06/15/02). Retrieved from the Worldwide Web: http://www.openmind.org/Articles/5g.htm.

Chapter 4: Specific Phobia

1. Reprinted with permission from the *Diagnostic and Statistical Manual of Mental Disorders,* Fourth Edition, Text Revision. Copyright 2000, American Psychiatric Association.

2. Satcher, David, M.D., Ph.D., Surgeon General, (1999) *Mental Health: A*

Report from the Surgeon General: Chapter 4. 10/09/02. Washington, D.C.: U.S. Government Printing Office, Retrieved from the Worldwide Web: http://surgeongenral.gov/library/mentalhealth/chapter4/sec2.html.
3. Reprinted with permission from the *Diagnostic and Statistical Manual of Mental Disorders,* Fourth Edition, Text Revision. Copyright 2000, American Psychiatric Association.
4. Discovery Health Features, 02/01/02, *Fires of the Mind: Specific Phobias.* 10/10/02. Retrieved from the Worldwide Web: http://health.discovery.com/convergence/fires/anxiety7.html.
5. Foana, Enda B., Jonathan R.T. Davidson, MD, Allen Frances, MD., and Ruth Ross, MA. Journal of Clinical Psychiatry, 1999; 60, (supl 16.) *Expert Consensus and Treatment for Posttraumatic Stress Disorder: A Guide for Patients and Families,* 1.

Chapter 5: Posttraumatic Stress Disorder

1. Reprinted with permission from the *Diagnostic and Statistical Manual of Mental Disorders,* Fourth Edition, Text Revision. Copyright 2000, American Psychiatric Association.
2. National Center for Post-Traumatic Stress Disorder, 06/13/00. *Epidemiological Facts About PTSD.* 10/10/02. Retrieved from Worldwide Web: http://www.ncptsd.org/facts,genral/fs-epdemilogical.html.
3. ibid.
4. ibid.
5. Grant, Robert, *Missisology: An International Review.* Vol. XXII. No. 1, January 1995. "Trauma in Missionary Life."
6. Reprinted with permission from the *Diagnostic and Statistical Manual of Mental Disorders,* Fourth Edition, Text Revision. Copyright 2000, American Psychiatric Association.
7. ibid.
8. Satcher, David, M.D., Ph.D., Surgeon General, (1999) *Mental Health: A Report from the Surgeon General:* Chapter 4. 10/09/02. Washington, D.C.: U.S. Government Printing Office, Retrieved from the Worldwide Web: http://surgeongenral.gov/library/mentalhealth/chapter4/sec2.html.

Chapter 6: Panic Disorder

1. Reprinted with permission from the *Diagnostic and Statistical Manual of Mental Disorders,* Fourth Edition, Text Revision. Copyright 2000, American Psychiatric Association.
2. Chandler, Jim, MD, (06/20/02). *Panic Disorder, Separation Anxiety Disorder, and Agoraphobia in Children and Adolescents.* Retrieved from the Worldwide Web: http://www.klis.com/chandler/pamphlet/panic/part1.htm.
3. National Institute of Mental Health. (1999). *Facts About Panic Disorder* (NIMH Publication No. OM-99 4155 revised,) Bethesda, MD.
4. PsychNet, APA, HelpCenter, n.d. *How Therapy Helps, Get the Facts:*

Answers to Your Questions About Panic. 10/09/02. Retrieved from the Worldwide Web: http://helping.apa.org/therapy/panic.html.
5. ibid.
6. Reprinted with permission from the *Diagnostic and Statistical Manual of Mental Disorders*, Fourth Edition, Text Revision. Copyright 2000, American Psychiatric Association.
7. ibid.
8. Satcher, David, M.D., Ph.D., Surgeon General, (1999) *Mental Health: A Report from the Surgeon General:* Chapter 4. 10/09/02. Washington, D.C.: U.S. Government Printing Office, Retrieved from the Worldwide Web: http://surgeongenral.gov/library/mentalhealth/chapter4/sec2.html.

Chapter 7: Obsessive Compulsive Disorder

1. Reprinted with permission from the *Diagnostic and Statistical Manual of Mental Disorders*, Fourth Edition, Text Revision. Copyright 2000, American Psychiatric Association.
2. Bourne, Edmund, Ph.D., *The Anxiety & Phobia Workbook*, (Third Edition), New Harbinger Publications, Inc, Oakland, CA. (2000), 367.
3. Reprinted with permission from the *Diagnostic and Statistical Manual of Mental Disorders*, Fourth Edition, Text Revision. Copyright 2000, American Psychiatric Association.
4. *Webster's New Encyclopedic Dictionary*, (1994). New York, NY.
5. National Anxiety Foundation, nd. *Obsessive Compulsive Disorders.* 10/10/02. Retrieved from the Worldwide Web: http://lexington-on-line.com/naf.ocd.2.html.
6. ibid.
7. Reprinted with permission from the *Diagnostic and Statistical Manual of Mental Disorders*, Fourth Edition, Text Revision. Copyright 2000, American Psychiatric Association.
8. National Institute of Mental Health. (1999). *Facts About Obsessive-Compulsive Disorder*, (NIMH Publication No. 99-3755 revised, 09/96) Bethesda, MD. NIH.
9. ibid.
10. ibid.

Chapter 8: Deep Breathing and Other Relaxation Techniques

1. *Webster's New Encyclopedic Dictionary*, (1994). New York, NY.

Chapter 9: Systematic Desensitization

1. *Webster's New Encyclopedic Dictionary*, (1994). New York, NY.
2. *Webster's New Encyclopedic Dictionary*, (1994). New York, NY.
3. Bourne, Edmund, Ph.D., *The Anxiety & Phobia Workbook*, (Third Edition), New Harbinger Publications, Inc, Oakland, CA, (2000).

Index

For additional information about Carol's counseling practice, speaking, or additional resources, please contact:

Carol M. Christensen, MA, LMHC
P.O. Box 102
Edmonds, Washington 98020
(206) 517–3843
www.carolchristensen.com